An Armless Hand Writes

A Collection of Poems

K.K. Srivastava

ATLANTIC

PUBLISHERS & DISTRIBUTORS (P) LTD

Published by

ATLANTIC

PUBLISHERS & DISTRIBUTORS (P) LTD

7/22, Ansari Road, Darya Ganj,
New Delhi-110002
Phones : +91-11-40775252, 23273880, 23275880, 23280451
Fax : +91-11-23285873
Web : www.atlanticbooks.com
E-mail : orders@atlanticbooks.com

Branch Office
5, Nallathambi Street, Wallajah Road,
Chennai-600002
Phones : +91-44-64611085, 32413319
E-mail : chennai@atlanticbooks com

Printed in India at Nice Printing Press, A-33/3A, Site-IV, Industrial Area, Sahibabad, Ghaziabad, U.P.

Contents

Preface

Over men intelligent and yeah, yeah, I have not forgotten as I hasten to add, over women beautiful, such being the uniqueness of their prodigious grandeur, that much ink has been spilt in the history and much will continue to be spilt in times to come by writers of all ilk making history replete with glorified and splendid deeds and misdeeds of such men and such women; the deeds and misdeeds, alive forever on the lips of posterity; and although I have no lofty intentions of making forays into the irresistible reservoir of their intelligence and beauty as I rate myself extremely ill-equipped in attempting any estimate, not to talk of judicial estimate, of such worthies (both sexes) yet my pious/honest job of writing bestows on me a responsibility that I proceed to discharge now and discharge this I will by reminding myself that I have never quenched my thirst with the water from the glass filled from Lethe's wharf.[1] Most of the human follies and vices, those who believe in the painful and oftentimes inenubilable tyrannies and treacheries of history and I trust, there being no dearth of such ardent believers, such believers will tend, without much cavil and reserve; without being unduly perturbed by what they may consider as jejunely stimulating nature of an opinion as is being expressed here; and without letting the immunity of their unmolested belief about such men and women fall a victim to jingled vagaries of their benevolent minds, to believe in it too, are committed by men who, notwithstanding their vociferous refusal to acknowledge it, consider themselves of more elevated minds and intelligence than they actually are and by women, again notwithstanding their ignorance of the causes of such follies, more beautiful than

[1] Lethe, a river in the underworld. Anyone drinking water from this river will suffer from forgetfulness.

they actually are; and further continuing with this opinion, much to our chagrin and mortification, these follies and vices, instead of being held in dread, get, eulogies of the first water, gigantic accolade and accord; approbation of highest order, which towards the end satisfy all the genuine criteria needed to prove the proverb, "Much ado about nothing" true. Oblivious, as, I am not of my primary responsibility towards readers, let me make it abundantly clear that in undertaking the present enterprise, I will allow my usual wisdom not to classify me in the league of such intelligent men; and to curious readers would emerge follies, my very own or of my own creation, in this writing, for which my apologies are placed before them, as people say, well in advance.

I regret. Why this first paragraph? Is it needed, particularly when I have not even laid my cards on the table? Is it because there are "little puny critics, who scatter their peevish strictures in private circles...*with* a patulence and illiberality in their remarks, which should place them as far beneath the notice of a gentleman as their original dullness had sunk them from the level of the most unsuccessful author"?[2] I am really at a loss to dilate upon what Sheridan says. The best judge is the reader. I leave it at that: as wise readers will, of course, draw their own conclusions as to the real motive behind it. I, for one, would say my desire not to sail under false colours has tempted me to pen this; the very first paragraph. I have tried my best not to leave any scope for unexplained ejaculations that make the meaning of what I have stated above as unintelligible and thus there is no need to belabour this issue any further.

And as a part of honest confession, let it be mentioned in the beginning itself, I have absolutely no idea as to where would what I write ultimately head me to. "Where, then, shall I be brought?" These words of Kafka while he wondered contemplating where his words would lead him, have haunted writers, historically as well as contemporarily, confronting them with a sort of inexplicable dilemma which assumes a more

[2] R.B. Sheridan in his Preface to *The Rivals*. (italics mine)

pronounced form in case of poets. This dilemma, perhaps, is a poet's greatest strength, for it confers on a poet a sense of intellectual detachment, at times transcendent and naïve, at times awful; and with this sense he writes his *art poetique*, amid ambiguous, sardonic and dusky anonymity/obscurity and self-effacement about the ideas that go into making of his poems. Ideas and their overwhelming, abstract silence, with myriad of structural elements factored in as poets are seized as they progress recording these ideas, mingling these with images, and creating what Jorge Luis Borges calls a maze of forking paths from which several realities may flow.

Words and ideas rarely make excellent bed-fellows but when they do what happens none can summarize better than Hazlitt, "my ideas float on winged words, as they expand their plumes, catch the golden light of other years.... Poetry and Philosophy had met together. Truth and Genius had embraced."[3] But alas! Poets are still not rescued ones. Nothing rescues them; not even words, brave words, not even ideas. An idea like a word is alive not because it is not dead but because it is alive because what is alive is alive not because it is not dead. Do ideas and words form thought process? To this question, I turn now by putting forth another question, "Can our thought apprehend the nature of thought?". This is a question to which was sought an introspective report by Buhler, a psychologist in 1907. And in the introspective report that emerged; this is what is to be taken note of—"I knew at the moment precisely what the whole thing was about; there were no words in it, though, and there were no ideas either." This question and more relevantly the response to this question retains its paramount importance when thought over in the context of ideas, ideas that writers deal with while writing. Ideas do infatuate me as they do other writers. Ideas, in form, embryonic, swinging between limits—uncertain, undefined, unstructured, incoherent, formless and at times, nonexistent; convey to me images not always clear and straightforward but oftentimes jumbled and fragmented ones.

[3] Hazlitt's essay "My First Acquaintance With Poets."

Only precondition I put forth before myself, while assessing these ideas as reasonable or otherwise, is that these ideas must be formed of indissoluble substance, capable of self-reflexion, self-doubts and be in a position to grapple with the philosophical issues (reflecting on the philosophies of the flux) that deal with complex relationships between the whole and the parts and *vice versa* and yet more complex relationship between cohesive primordial instincts and incohesive and errant reason running beneath sophistication lacking both in intellect and intuition. This, in turn, places on me an onerous responsibility: reading ideas, particularly those characterized by presence/absence of psychic conflicts/maturity. Such ideas do have traits of opposites wherefrom a writer derives his *raison d'être* for his indulgence in writings, which sometimes do border on bewildering assortment of absurdities that seem to be rolling unbridled. World, being a supra-personal-psychic fact, is not bereft of such absurdities is a fact, hard to dispute.

Then, can we say ideas can explain relations on their own? Are ideas relationless? If not brought within the ambit of discussion, related or interconnected phenomena: concept formation, insight, cognition, sensations, impulses, judgment, memory, associations—free or restrained, imagery etc., the discussion would lead us nowhere. Poetry both as a static concept as well as a continuous process involves an intensive and extensive use of all these mental events, which in turn have their own methodological complexities. A poet's perception of issues thus is a perception, continuously regulated by these mental processes. Mozart ignorance as to "Whence and how they (ideas) come, I know not; nor can I force them" is not his ignorance alone; it is the collective ignorance of almost all the writers, particularly poets because poets, serious poets, do wade through as much obscurity of their thought process knowing not the inner details of exploratory mechanism at work when they pen their lines as no other brand of writers does. The exploratory processes typically have five components: observation, selection, scrutiny, analysis and reporting, all parts of the elemental process having linkages to consciousness. And when I say consciousness, someone may butt in and say, "What about unconsciousness?" A fair question to be answered fairly but to which I will revert later. For the present, mark the words uttered by Mozart. "Whence and when they come." These take me to that realm of mind where melting of consciousness and unconsciousness and *vice versa* takes place. The linkages may be naïve but not devoid of, at least always, of predetermined structures. Puzzles set in for poets as early as they perceive objects in their most primitive, structural form. A poet struggles to reach out to an idea in terms of clear images that further have the support of concepts, which need not necessarily be logically connected. Thus a poet's search for logical connections in the images he explores in order to write his poems may not be certain to succeed. The greatest problem a poet faces in his interaction with images is the presence of many imageless thoughts (imageless thoughts, as I construe these, can be interpreted to connote a situation when you are not able to respond in a coherent manner: you have no idea whether your conscious has sensations or images or both.) making his creative life a hotbed of incoherent images/sensations wherein he dips himself repeatedly to cull out some meaningful associations. Laski in his letter to Russel writes "Many thanks for the photograph. Even if it is bad, it gives a basis to the imagination...."[4] I don't get a better example than this: a bad photograph akin to imageless thought. Thus, a poet has no easy task before him: he is confronted with imageless thoughts that make it difficult for him to reproduce the output of his thought process which having dealt with the primary inputs about the external world (a photograph); inputs he looks at in a detached, snarled manner to clothe his ideas with words, propels him to move somewhere else: to clamber up the difficult monoliths towards the basis to (the imagination). Think of an object, you have not seen; you are hearing about it for the first time or you have not even heard of it; you have not even read anything

---

[4] Harold J. Laski in his letter dated 2nd November 1919 to Bertrand Russell as quoted in Bertrand Russell's *Autobiography*.

about it. How would you go about describing that object, if need be? This is a dilemma a poet faces: dilemma of expanding a thought that has not come to him with words but for which he has to introduce words and he knows not if the words really explain that nebulous thought, that imageless thought: that thought which has no words, leaving the poet with no choice but to resort to the process of what is called "d'edoublement". What constitute "d'edoublement"?

Let me revert back to the issue raised earlier: unconsciousness. Let us focus on crisscrossing lines of consciousness, superimposing unconsciousness upon what seems to be real, at least to the eyes. But what seems to be real to a poet may dissolve into figureless reality if no aid accrues from unconsciousness; if the closed circuits of consciousness continue to firm up their grip over unconsciousness. This is where writers resort to "d'edoublement". It simply means alternation: a writer as "I" is on the stage and the characters or objects he is tackling are in the backdrop, of course, for a while and then suddenly the scene changes; characters/objects come to the center-stage, the "I" in the writer withdraws or retreats, again for a while. Thus, the "I" is struggling with itself. Sometimes the "I" is conscious; sometimes unconscious; sometimes the absence of "I" is conscious and sometimes unconscious; a circleless relationship is underway. Self is split but it is not a case of split personality. It is a link between what are split. What is private is private but what is open also absorbs in it what is private. This brings us to the moot point. What happens to the relationship between "I" and the characters/objects is important but equally important are how and why things happen to that relationship as a poet proceeds with filling the blank pages. Functional relationship among various happenings/events in the mind of a poet are the *sine qua non* for a poet as within those functional relationships lie both the background and the figure of serious poetic thoughts: a poet searches unique relationships between background and figure. This functional relationship a poet can present as a single-peaked entity as in a short poem or as a multiple-peaked entity as in very long poems and it are in latter, a poet has to adopt the technique of "d'edoublement". This facilitates achievement of yet another objective. Unity in a long poem: one sequence as a whole; all segregated thoughts fused together, is achieved. After all, any poet hopes to achieve an intuitive grasp of the overall value of an experience or feeling or sensation and this experience, this feeling, this sensation emerges from something, from somewhere which is abundantly obscure and befuddling. This is an issue I will touch later. A poet, suddenly seized with a desire to describe a beautiful face of a beautiful woman that he saw, from very close quarters, a decade back but that still haunts him though, intermittently, cannot describe it adequately unless he is able to create a structural relationship between what he observes in that face and what is his other experience: the other experience acting like background and the face as figure: his poem is nothing but a description of intellectual atmosphere obtaining between the figure and the background and explaining the relationship between the two.

Husserl[5], perhaps it was, who called this relationship, "noema". Wood also is to be seen; not the tree alone. Husserl takes us further: he talks of empty intentions and fulfilled intentions. This is where I get the best definition of poetry; serious poetry: it is nothing but a bridging of the gap between empty intentions and fulfilled intentions.[6]

In such situations, what fills in the details and what helps writers who adopt this technique in formation of ideas is what forces them to creep into the realms of unconscious. Unconscious implies that portion of psyche which stores forgotten, repressed memories/fantasies/desires which don't reveal themselves directly to conscious but may get manifested under hypnosis or may come in dreams. It is important to note that things hidden in unconscious tend to move outward and psychiatrists believe

[5] Husserl as quoted in the essay, "Reflecting on the pre-reflective: Phenomenology" by Neil Bolton.

[6] Expanding on the example I have given earlier, a poet sees a face and desires to kiss it: it is an empty intention. He actually kisses it (and I tell myself not all are lucky), it is a fulfilled intention.

that an individual achieves "wholeness" only when images, fantasies, and dreams from his personal and collective memories become accessible to the conscious self.

Dreams are important (Freud refers to their interpretation as "via regia" to a knowledge of unconscious): they provide to a poet an array of associations, that he may, subject to his emotional and intellectual capabilities, involving an endless sorting and recombining of knowledge, observations and speculations, use in linking with things he has seen, noticed or felt. The problem extends and expands itself. This linking is neither continuous nor smooth nor complete (continuity and smoothness, being important criteria for coming out of a period of "perplexity or quite", call forth subtlety of insights that might be straying ones), for there are gaps, the gaps; the inevitable, elusive gaps, a poet has to fill with inferences. Dreams bring with them plethora of multi-peaked, incomprehensible, inpenetratable, masked issues that visit a poet along with gaps when he is writing. And whatever comes to him would be having serious implications in terms of content, entirety, complexities, conceitedness, involuntariness, than what stay with him in his waking consciousness. Associations are important; associations that emerge as definite pattern from the dream but extremely difficult to have their linkages clearly established *vis a vis* realities of the day. Let us have a look at two dreams.

The first one. Freud[7] refers to the dream of a young girl who saw in her dream that the second son of her sister died under the same circumstances in which died the first son. On waking up, she found it hard to accept it as it was never her wish to see her sister's second son's death. On analysis, it emerged that the young girl had, on the occasion of the death of the first son of her sister, met the man she adored the most. And it was to meet him again; she saw that nasty, discomforting dream. Here, thus association is with suppressed desires: to meet the man she liked.

---

[7] Freud in *On Dreams* (chapter IX).

The second one. "I was walking down the street and I saw this booth and it said 'help fat people'...and it was full of ugly, fat people. I would be interested in finding out what this fatness is, ah, what it represents, ah, 'help ugly fat people reduce', it said. 'Pay here and we will give you the means or something like this.' So I went up and paid a lot of money and, ah, went away.... That was the end of the dream."

Breger[8] reports this dream of a girl; and on analysis of associations, it came to notice that the girl secretly had an abortion and she lost the child. The 'ugly' aspects of fat people in the dream have been equated with the guilt she felt over her pregnancy and abortion.

Thus human contacts, relationships with things so visible, so invisible, so apparent, fluctuating, agile, dead, penetrate a poet's mind when he is with himself, pondering over these relationships, trying to arrive at equations that would accost him, continually, during his activated thought process, and that would ultimately transform themselves into verse. This part of association with things, mundane, hidden and structured, poses no great problems for a poet, for contacts and relationships are immutably overpowered by the imaginative skills a poet possesses. Nothing is sub-rosa, here. Fortunately.

What I am trying to drive at is the inevitable fact that contact with reality, while leading to some of the most remarkable themes for poetry, need not be the only themes that are integrated into conscious. A lot lie there beneath mounds and mounds of inaccessible parts of psyche and the difficult job that falls on a poet is akin to that of Geoffrey Chaucer's army that had to drag "out of the heap of the dead", the two knights, Arcita and Palamon,"who were not quite alive nor wholly dead". Like Arcita and Palamon, these activities of unconscious mind, more often than not, are neither "quite alive nor wholly dead" rendering the job of a poet as difficult as Chaucer's army

[8] I. Breger in the article, 'Function of dreams'.

men who had to "drag forth" these two out of "the heap of the dead".[9]

A poet never starts his voyage with tabula rasa. It is the nascence of immediate cause for provocation for a thought, however innocuous looking or harmless it might be, that primarily prompts a poet to initiate himself in his venture but the association of accumulated experiences which set the initial idea or the immediate experience in a blaze continuing throughout his poem or sometimes even after the poem is completed is no less unique. In poems that are quite long and that have witnessed many paradigms emanating from the poet's personality, these associations get broken many times making the poem incomprehensible.

What I started with in the very beginning, I have not talked of so far. Let me mend my ways. Men and women: those intelligent and beautiful creatures of the world, their incorrigible relationship, their amorphous ties, their essence or effects on essence of these relationships, these ties have attracted the attention of writers of all sorts, over ages, and copious literature has come into being, bearing on the complexities of these relationships/ties. Exploring various themes underlying that relationship and mental perceptions governing the known world within the unknown one and *vice versa* transports a poet to uniqueness of its own, where psychic imagination has to go hand in hand with poetical selectivity and sensitivity, all shifting concurrently or variously. When we look at these relationships, having symbolic and mystical patterns, combining women's purity with passion, ideals with reality: all startling and disturbing men, we feel that defenses of a poet are meagerly equipped to deal with insufficiencies of input coming his way, insufficiencies deeply rooted in what are normally perceived as contradictions of the highest order. Pablo Neruda touches this sensitive relationship (and having read these lines of Neruda, I really marvel at this sensitive relationship) between men and women with his philosophical erudition,

---

[9] The Knight's *Tale by Geoffrey Chaucer.*

"They say terrible things
about a man and a woman
who, after much milling about,
all sorts of compunctions,
do something unique—
they both lie with each other in one bed."[10]

Different scholars have different experiences. Bernard Shaw (a bachelor) shares another problem with his readers. Why people, broods he, constantly attached to the "hideous witches" of Macbeth yawn at the prospect of spending an evening with a beauteous lady possessing what Shaw calls, "voluptuous contours"?[11] This strange phenomenon concerning men-women relationship is not only baffling and obfuscating for Shaw alone but also for poets world over and act as a great temptation for these poets to delve into intricacies of such relations before they portray their understanding of these relations in their verses.

Emotions and emotional distortions, both having inner life the way they do have an outer one-a revealed one (I have yet not ceased talking of men-women relationships) bring with them immense solace of one kind or the other. These allow poets a luxurious indulgence in poetical possibilities, leading to a state of imaginative equilibrium: a state of vitalizing incompleteness, a drift towards infinite nothingness because the fragmented, the disintegrated emotion and emotional distortions represent an indivisible continuum. Those acquainted with the works, for example, of Shakespeare.[12] D.H. Lawrence[13] and Derek Walcott[14] would agree that when they draw a parallel between moon and a woman (Why? Can you hazard a guess? Of course,

---

[10] 'Poor Fellows' by Pablo Neruda.

[11] George Bernard Shaw in preface to *The Devil's Disciple*.

[12] Recall Othello's words, "you are welcome, sir, to Cyprus-Goats and Monkeys!" Goats and Monkeys have been used to interpret lust. *Othello* (Act 4/Scene 1)

[13] *Women in Love* by D.H. Lawrence.

[14] *Goats and Monkeys* by Walcott.

I know but am not inclined to share this exciting knowledge with you), they convey an idea. For a poet, moon and woman are symbolic; a woman creating abstract ideas in poet's mind and unnerving him, at least, sometimes. Look at these lines,

> "The feelings I don't have I don't have.
> ....
> The feelings you say you have, you don't have.
> ....
> So if you want either of us to feel anything at all
> You'd better abandon all idea of feelings altogether."[15]

Longing for a woman and using it creatively to undermine important sensuous or emotional requirements are what poets normally try to achieve through their poems and in this process, startlingly extravagant experiences and their lonely self-scrutiny and the rigours of long journeys have to be encountered to narrate these experiences, unscathed and at times under oblique inertia.

Overall unity and scheme of poems (I come to an issue raised earlier), longer ones, in particular, pose problems both of form and content not only when we look at the way, poems evolve over a period of time and get written (sometimes a long poem can take six months or even more) but also how these absorb various influences, simple to complex, facile to comprehensive, the poet has received in the past as also what he receives while he pens the poem. What is the exact procedure at work can never be the same for different practitioners of the game of poetic creation but by and large the contours call for an adherence, albeit, flexible one, to a plain, inhibiting restlessness ceasing to enjoy the truth/falsehood of its insides, trying, intermittently, its hands at remaking, retelling, reconnoitering its own experiences and wondering deliriously. There may be ideas, functioning in isolation; these are not of much relevance to a poet. Ideas that transcend beyond concerns of immanent immediacy necessitating the poets to sublime what surrounds

[15] 'To Women, as far as I'm concerned' by D.H. Lawrence.

them in their immediate and short run circumstances into concerns of interior consciousness that do not stick to the flux of that world where poets hunger for mundane things like poverty, diseases, divorces, dirt, squalor, taverns, temples, riots etc, are the ideas that enthrall some poets. Best literature would have died long back, had poets not sought a departure from these mundane issues and voyaged in the direction of exploring things, unique and unpoetic.

As for myself, most of the ideas coming to me adopt not the main route but usually the detour, and I never consider it as something that places limitations on my ability to comprehend and compress different ideas, despite their complexities and varieties, before I try to mould these into the shape of poems and in so doing my desire for metaphysically restless ideas never ceases to rest. What perhaps happens to be the most unmistakable characteristic of these ideas is not only the intricate relationships they are enjoying with the external environment they stem from but also the murkier background of the unconscious they are seething with. Things don't stay so easy. Are the ideas we are talking about real or are these abstract or do these combine traits of both? One of the greatest philosophers Benedict de Spinoza's[16] prescription of a system of interlocking of various ideas offers yet another instrument in the hands of poets to correlate the genesis of a particular idea, irrespective of whether it crops up from external environment or otherwise, with other ideas existing, not necessarily physically but psychically. For Spinoza, even if an idea is distinct and clear, it has it's existence but we cannot trace out it's connections with other ideas. If a thing is having no connections with other things, that thing is an abstraction. What a poet ought to understand, at this point of time, is that the recourse to the route mentioned above has a high and spruced-up demand associated with it, a demand that

[16] Having cast the whole world in the form of geometric theorem, Spinoza, makes it static and proceeds on to prove that from something, everything else can be shown to follow necessarily: if a thing be true it must ensue from the whole reality. Thus ideas are interlocked.

requires complete adherence to one's intellectual integrity which further has got to be intuitively and instinctively harmonized into his perception of the delicate dualism between central or core idea *vis a vis* innumerable other ideas, most of which happen to be inscrutable from different angles.

The inseparability of central core from the rest needs an elucidation and the most appropriate example I can give is to cite an illustration from Erich Fromm.[17] When a six-year-old child tells his mother, writes Fromm, "I love you" he conveys his experience at the age of six. Repetition of the same to a young lady when the same child is twenty years old conveys, in the words of Fromm, "different meaning, expressing the wider range, the greater depth, the larger freedom and activity". What is important here to note is that the word "love" has a common core though the experience to which it refers is different in the child and in the man. Similarly, child and young man are different from each other still they are the same.

A poet dealing with this core idea and other associated ideas is required to have a thought process that involves imagination, realities, application of formal logic to thinking, retrieval from memory, all requiring setting rules of reference that allow drawing of conclusions from underlying logical assumptions in a manner that is valid but that has an inbuilt mechanism to confront the poet with twin tasks i.e. interpretational and operational. The former deals with poet's comprehension of various core/central ideas and the latter; his ability to carry out reasoning operations meant to uncap the hidden appearances forming the warp and woof of these core ideas and from these warp and woof of core ideas, a poet picks up associated ideas. A continual process, mixing parts with the whole and *vice versa*, a kaleidoscopic process propelling immanent realities towards the clouds of unknowing where only the inner experiences can get an opening, duly confronted with elevated planes of unconsciousness necessitating reworking of one idea itself but not necessarily immune from the cosmos of innumerable realities

[17] Erich Fromm's *You Shall Be As Gods.*

riddled with contradictions both, internal and external, is underway. And as F.H. Bradley rightly points out realities are much more than "impalpable abstractions, or unearthly ballet of bloodless categories". and further that whatever is the immediate experience, it is nothing but one unitary experience, not yet parted by any relation and distinction. He gives us an example. We are in total darkness hung over a stream and look down on it. There are no banks in the stream and its current is filled with floating images, a continuous process. There is a bright-illumined spot on the water, which ceaselessly widens and narrows its area, thus showing what passes away on the current. This spot is what Bradley calls our present. The rest of the stream is total darkness. A paler light, both up and down stream, is shed on what comes before and after now. This paler light, Bradley calls, offspring of the present.[18] This perhaps is the best relationship between the core idea and associated ideas. This immediate experience, as a poet tackles it, when he starts expanding it, troubles him in as much as it is not only the nascent nature of that experience but also the variants of experiences that he has accumulated over a great length of time and the effect of the nature and structure of the influence on the immediate experience that he has to lump together with a view to express himself candidly. This immediate totality of perception is the most important aspect that ought to be sustained through a careful working of the relationship between immediate experience and its further refinement by the poet. No escapement is possible. And readers too, more often than not, are tempted by their immediate experience while reading a line and they add enhanced value of their interpretation, that is nothing but a consequence of their accumulated and more importantly personal possession of their experiences, to their immediate experience. Things beyond truth, beauty and love fascinate poets. A re-look at most of the poems adds further to the chaos emerging from abstractions that have no value, so it seems. Is it because poets fail to integrate all that come to them, from various sources,

[18] F.H. Bradley in *The Principles Of Logic.*

signifying various things, contradictory most of the times and choking one time or the other? There are so many odds poets are pitted against and what confuses them further is their lack of realization of these oddities.

This is, in brief, my understanding of poetry. I may be totally wrong but as of now, I go by what I have written above as I believe; futility of an opinion does not alienate opinion from opinion-holders.

Before I round off this preface, another horrendous job awaits me; not of making acknowledgements (of course, it can never be horrendous) but of ordering the priorities. Seeing so many acknowledgements, commencing with the role wives of writers play in their husbands' creative achievements, I, at times, wonder what would have happened to the ever growing world of literary achievements, had these wives not been there. That settles the question of priorities for me.

First and foremost, my high and deep respect to those schoolteachers who taught me, amidst their poverty, in dilapidated rooms of municipal schools of Gorakhpur, an unformed district in eastern Uttar Pradesh (I am talking of early sixties), the art of thinking and writing—the art of toying with ideas, nascent ideas and nascent words. What I learnt from them is something invaluable, which is acknowledged here. Thanks to my late uncle (a teacher in an intermediate college) who gave me the world of books and introduced me to the habit of reading books, a habit, fortunately, I continue with even now. I owe a very deep acknowledgement to all the poets/review writers/ friends both from this country and abroad: the persons I have never met, never talked but who have appreciated my first book of poems. In particular, I am indebted to the celebrated, reclusive poet Jayanta Mahapatra who despite his age of 79, responded to each and every letter of mine and I get a message as to how hard is the road ahead and how a sense of detachment is required for writing poetry. Your kind words, Sir, will guide me, throughout.

We know people don't read poetry; serious poetry at that. But then surprises from unexpected quarters can hail a poet. That lazy, frowsty afternoon, dusk not too far, someone (on two persons agreeing to have undefined relations that I rate as most valued relations between two human beings, both names and identities lose relevance), dropped in and discussed some of my poems from my earlier book and conveyed to me observations on these poems and also on some of the sample poems for my present book. The observations helped me, to some extent, in reaching out to some of my sequestered ideas. Nowadays, when courtesies, particularly among youth are becoming a rarer phenomenon, though many adults (both sexes), intellectually-fossilized ones, also show abundance of wide and varied discourtesies, day in, day out; the courtesy shown by this intelligent person (of course, I am aware of the tribe of disputants who, as is their wont, dispute and question, as they would have done in any other case, my capabilities to judge someone's intelligence; and to such disputants I will only tell that having lived forty-seven years of one's life, one should have adequate capabilities and faculties to have a fair idea as to who are intelligent and who are not. I, definitely, have this idea. No qualms about it. And I am prepared to be dubbed a megalomaniac) was remarkable which is acknowledged.

And for my family, I go by what I recorded in my earlier book, Ineluctable Stillness and this is what I find there "No writer can ever afford to ignore the role, his family plays in the creation of his works.... No sensible person will ever deny that but for the active cooperation of the family, not to speak of creative work, even most simple works can be done. I thank my wife and two sons, who, though they could never get themselves rid of their lurking doubts about the utility and futility of my activities in hand, equipped me with a congenial and peaceful atmosphere inside the house, a *sine qua non* for a beginner like me." Opinion intact.

And to my prospective readers, I will urge only one thing. Please read this book but never, never with the expectation of having an experience that befell that great writer after he consumed opium, the experience so beautifully summed up:

"...O heavens! what a revulsion! what a resurrection, from its lowest depths of the inner spirit! what an apocalypse of the world within me."[19]

I know no poetry can have such a devastating effect: poetry is never meant for that.

Jaipur **K.K. Srivastava**

[19] *Confessions Of An English Opium-Eater* by Thomas De Quincey.

I

(For those, unable to step out of themselves)

I am I,
a farrago of heap, gargantuan,
of myself.
Aglow with my colossus vanity,
driven by my monstrous
avalanche
towards my ambitions,
I, in-kneed before my impuissant ego.

Plunging into deeps and shoals of thoughts
about myself,
I have killed my emotions,
and succumbed to my servitudes.
And thus, have swallowed last drops of shame.
I reject the echoes from the rational
world,
I, one with the lemurs, who talk my language,
I, a part of limping
stories that gaze, helplessly,
into anfractuous shadows.

I am I.
Hidden,
quiescent vultures blind
my faith in my interior being.
I, a multivalent crowd of myself, making me
mad and ugly but
acceptable.

Not quivering before illogic,
I do yield to unrealities

toying with bigger unrealities.
Wearing numerous looks,
I nauseate intellectually
amid my resonating voice.
And search, desperately, the one in me.
Barabas, Barabas, Barabas,[1]
deeply embedded.

I am I,
with neither sense nor sensibility,
neither vision nor grace,
still I explore within my explosions,
hopelessly agile and helplessly
awful.
I have a delightfully active "I"
purring to me, incessantly,
about my frowning ego,
never going tippy.

I have neither "greatest completeness, with
all the incidental consequences" nor do I have
"entire truthfulness"[2]
still my "self-perception" hounds me
as does hound an eagle a rat.

My arrogance,
groovy,
deranges me so pathetically,
I live,
continually,
amid my life alone,

---

[1] Barabas, in *The Jew of Malta* by Christopher Marlowe, avers, "Ego mihimet sum semper proximus", the translation of which, as mentioned in the book is, "no man is nearer friend to myself than I am." (1.1)

[2] Franz Kafka's Diary 1911 emphasizes fulfillment of above conditions in order to shun betraying of "self-perception".

flickering, occasionally,
calmed down by the fury within.

I have a buried conscience
ejaculating about itself
as I stay awake,
and again about itself,
as slumber steals upon me,
realizing not "people being naturally full
of themselves when they have nothing else in themselves."[3]

I am I,
unstirred within my mental torpor,
fabulously piteous,
but perfectly caged, firmly,
within the frills of my orotund, dead shadow.

---

[3] From Joseph Addison's essay "On Egotism". To those who, really stay, always, with themselves, I strongly recommend, not only this essay but also and more forcefully, Sigmund Freud's case study entitled, "On The Mechanism Of Paranoia" as published in his Case Histories, Volume 9, in which he demonstrates the linkages among "auto-erotism", "object-love", "ego-cathexes" , "megalomania" and "paranoia". Those who are obsessed with "I", are those who "linger unusually long" while being in half-way phase between "auto-erotism" and "object-love".

Serious Poetry, My Dear Phoebeans,[1] Is Not Schizophrenic Verbalism[2]

My dear friends,
Fellow-travelers.
Are we poets insane with our
imperfections?
Imperfections?
Goodness cheap in poetry
makes poetry brief in goodness.[3]
Imperfections and serious poetry?

Serious poetry, not a hollow myth,
descends like purring sensations,
fugaciously tiptoeing the unknowable
paths to unconquered vagaries of mind.

And thus
serious poetic impulses soberly invade
the poets from no where,
engaging them with incisive convolutions,
fixed in a timeless form.

For example, a serious poet would, at times,
go nostalgic and
wade through, in vain, sometimes lighter
and sometimes sober,

---

1 Phoebus, the God of poetry.

2 The relationship between metaphysics and poetry has evoked serious debate among philosophers and scholars. However, for Freud, metaphysics is tantamount to schizophrenic verbalism.

3 "[T]he goodness that is cheap in beauty, makes beauty brief in goodness...." so philosophizes the Duke to Isabella about beauty in Shakespeare's *Measure For Measure* (Act Three, Scene one).

Obscure ideas, unevenly placed,
rampageous, marauding aimlessly,
in the realm of lingering
intuitions,

Obstructed upheavals, ideals,
well-aroused, tormenting and extinguishing,
going astray in the realm of pultaceous
enquiries,

Obtruded wanderings around the slackening
abysses,
quiet dreams disconcerting the bliss,
outlines legion,
all sprawling together,

Oppressed enchantments, senseless and
azure,
innocent darkness relinquishing it's kindness,
fruitless desires reinforcing the disillusioned mind,
suddenly growing pale with fear,

Obsessed infatuation with objects,
terrestrials and extra-terrestrials,
heaving, dispassionately, through
the layers of unidentified corners of
the illumined mind.

Links between visible and invisible,
between temporal and ephemeral,
between escapable and inescapable,
between explicable and inexplicable
convulsing, floating and immersing.

Serious poetry,
a continuum
of echoing
muse, broken,

hazy and moiling
endeavoring
inanely to be
one with its own
reminiscences.

Serious poetry
begins where
recesses of conscious
and unconscious mind
start rolling
and discovering
each other,
together.

And, therefore,
serious poetry,
cognitive realism,
metaphysical
statements,
not really,
schizophrenic
verbalism.

Deep within our being
a deluge, spacious deluge makes a
medley of everything,
shriveling within
and make us, my dear poets,
yet other Phoebeans.

Love And Relationship

One day,
sitting there,
that place,
that vacant place,
I would answer your doubtings.

Love in relationship,
relationship in love
have no questions,
no answers.

Muteness and
their muteness alone
makes a questionless love
an answerless relationship,
an answerless relationship
a questionless love.

You still seek answers?

Oppressiveness Of Nothingness

1

Multiple planes we have been living on,
simultaneously,
the planes, indeterminate, dissolving,
exploring, combative and swinging.
We think and we feel,
we float between real and unreal,
between thoughtless visions
and thoughtful dreams.
We float between layers of instinct
and layers of reflection.
We float between alienation and nostalgia.
We float between intellect and
intuition.
We float between verisimilitude and
verity.
We sink in the quagmire of
forlorn hopes.
We float between absolutes and
postulates.
All these planes are the eras;
each era, "a beginning", not an "origin"
each having a "a task and a search".[1]
We do hobnob with ourselves
to reach a conclusion,
a conclusion about ourselves, our
intrinsic intensities, our delusive visions.

---

[1] Edward Said, in *Beginnings: Intention and Method*, differentiates between "beginning" and "origin" calling the former not "an achieved result" which is the case with the latter.

What stirs the historically squeezed
framework we ooze out from we know not
nor do we know the relations between the
human and the non-human; nor the individual
and the cosmos.

2

I wish I could have blank memory.
No nostalgia.
An infinitesimal imagery.
But what if these nasty erasures don't work now,
these are redundant and obscure,
these have left nothing to us.
I feel so oppressed.
I proceed with my vision blurred
and
traces of my identity unfurled.
Ensconced past and continuing present
traverse together sightlessly long,
thorny stretches,
stillness of travesties of raucous
past falls away.

3

Historical fallacies are deceitfully slime.
Where are the eyes you saw the dingy
pages of history through?
The chalice of memory,
not shakable for the present,
for ceremonial facts are not too far away
from equally ceremonial fictions.
History has its own breath,
you and I have, at times, wondered if
its breath has vicious breathlessness.
Don't you remember?
On that half-wintry morning

bulging imbecility visited us
as did visit a lashing, tumultuous,
spineless storm devastating everything
but us.

4

To discern the sobbing years that are
not with me now,
I plunged into glistening, shrinking
chasm-cracked depths of nothingness.
Elemental rudiments of left over past
came hopping,
disavowing their own liberation and
assimilating the time,
the indestructible
time, of late, terribly jerky to me.
Feasting on elongated threads of
kaleidoscopic days and nights,
evolving on the edge of wearisomely
fertile forgetfulness,
the thirsty shreds of oppression came
too near me,
fossilizing me,
for a while.
I stood aghast.
Not surprised.

5

The great poet-philosopher,
Pablo Neruda, reminds me of
his saddest lines that he penned
that night.[2]
What about my nights?
My night stays elusive,

---

[2] Neruda' poem, "Tonight I Can Write...."

my saddest thoughts have kept
me at bay so far.
Why I could not usurp my saddest
thoughts when she gave me my birth
or
when as a child I lost constantly
multiple battles
or
when she refused to acknowledge the
words she uttered when she and I were all alone
or
when I saw life bamboozling me, off and on.
Oppressiveness of nothingness.
You know what I mean to say.

6

Who would own him now?
Lousy men gossip aimlessly
flaunting their heroic deeds
and forgetting their unheroic misdeeds.
Charred monologues reveal
nothing, completely drowned
in elegant convulsions.
Let me crown him.
He loves to collapse, faced with
reverberating ceilings,
mental ones, I mean.
I never feel so oppressed as I feel now.
I wish I could merge with all
these illusory longings, deeds.
Alas! the dream is dead.

7

Broodingly melancholic,
I try to signify my poignancy
through a series of suffocating

rejections.
Then, through a series of frustrating affirmations.
My history keeps mum when these
rejections and affirmations do disown
me completely but shamefacedly.
On a road, a crawling road.
Empty roads no longer awe me.
These meet serene emptiness,
recoiling within my dead self.
I tell my beloved,
"My love for you is dead. It
is too late. I am busy in enlivening
my dead persona."
Gracefully, she deserts me.

8

That insignificant voice,
the mercifully insane voice,
the entreating voice,
the abysmally weary voice,
the girded voice,
the blinkingly bleak voice,
the wrinkled voice,
the yearning voice,
the scummy voice,
the exhausted voice,
having become revelatory of
it's feigning otherness, tells us,
in a hollow room,
that world is created,
"out of nothing"[3]
and it is this nothingness of "nothing"

[3] John Scotus Erigena, an Irish philosopher whose philosophical thoughts gave preference to emanation as compared to creation, believed that God created the world out of nothing. This "out of nothing" has been interpreted variously.

that oppresses
genuine minds.

9

Inside the depths of mine
cussed amnesia refuses to
stay in limbo.
A voice arises slowly
but someone scourges it.
I try to reach out to issues
that have started melting
even before these
could get firmed up.
Someone pulls me of my
seminally glowing
nothingness.
I feel so oppressed.
So depressed.

10

Ordained through the ungovernable
laws the cosmos had inherited,
reasons did conspire, again and again,
to hold unsurpassable consequences
to ransom.
I, a disbeliever in everything good and
sane, both cruel in measure equal,
sought indulgences in creative vibrations
coming my way, of course,
inadvertently.
The indulgences, glaring at eloping
uncertainties, told me plainly,
"Nothing oppresses more acutely than
nothingness of everything."
Waked thoughts vying with grim heavens.

11

Day-dreaming about the chaotic
obsessions, barren nerves decide
to go berserk,
for they are wrapped in the
vulnerable invincibility realities emanate from.
Elusive arousals tread carefully
the paths history has cluttered with
distorted perceptions.
Alternatives intermingle but the
outcome is intruding,
ambiguity becoming more precise.
Desires meet their demises
there, in the labyrinth of coils,
superimposing idealization over
harsh contours of realities as
we "dwelt alone In a world of moan,
And my soul was a stagnant tide."[4]

12

Cumbersome silence of fragmentary emotions
irks me like the silence of a dead man.
Internalization, internalization and internalization.
Ongoing process peeved at its own inertia.
That hunter of the east pontificates the death
of all that is delusion.
Delusions versus illusions,
outwardly silent worries mesmerizing me,
quenching fully my thirst for self-denials
but tempting me to add to my miseries.
Wisdom fails to strengthen me.
It weakens me.
Turbulences become immortal

---

[4] Edgar Poe in 'Eulalie – A Song'.

leaving pathways in a state of complete panic.
Solitude of oppressing nothingness hails me.

13

Deep ecstatic uprisings relinquish their
decaying innocence,
the intuition talks of jarring egos,
inner equanimity blossoms to the core.
Inclinations loiter around
the indistinct,
the dizzy,
frames realities have chosen to conceal.
I must have traveled on innumerable
dreams, the dreams that once upon a time,
transformed me into a wolf
but now the dreams come to me as wolves
like death coming to a starving child.
Mirrors don't reflect realities now,
these do reflect unseen dreams,
for, unseen dreams don't copulate
with seen realities.

14

The citadel, where the uncanny abilities,
the history stores, does hoodwink us,
and we allow it to hoodwink us into
disbelieving that there exists such a citadel.
We are seduced.
The citadel is farcical.
The citadel is exclusive.
Let us not search into it the uncreated
nightmares, tiny, wily, puny.
These nightmares come during daytime
now.

These come, as "WOTAN"[5] comes,
off and on, in our collective lives.
Brightness of the sky laments the blooming
of the earth.

15

Lackadaisical craziness ripping apart
the pretence of history,
the history you people keep so close
to your marrow, your blood and bones.
What for?
None knows.
Don't wallow in self-created mess.
You would be eaten away.
By your proximity to your past.
Time, the greatest dreamer of all dreams,
the greatest conjuror.
It sails unmercifully on the broken
edges of our past.
Shadows of oblivion still linger on.

16

Impulses are restrictive
but reflective.
They do dwell upon a life
that shimmers.
They also proclaim the victory
of withdrawn symbols over
perceptions defying interpretations.
Unceasingly,
beautifully,
the pleasures embedded in our misery-driven

[5] Wotan is a restless wanderer who creates unrest and aggravates strife. Carl Jung refers to this Wotan as "an autonomous psychic factor" affecting collective life in his essay titled 'Wotan'.

wishes push us towards severed perplexities
dawning upon mortals.
Bliss is never heavenly.
It need not be.
I am not tempted to alight on this bliss.
For, I am I, I am alive, I mimic no zombies.

17

Dichotomies, they say, are part of nothingness.
The rigours of history, vanishing swiftly,
cast their shadows on my vagrancy,
on my uprooted-ness.
I intend to turn rotten, for a while.
Unmeddled subtleties,
hissing and fuming,
have frozen me for good.
I intend to blind my eyes to elements
of my internal ruminations,
choking me, defrosting me slowly.
I have ceased to think,
for nothing pains more than what
constitutes the irresistibility of thoughtless
muses.

18

Look, look, there, not so far off,
there recurs, again, much to my chagrin,
willy-nilly flowing of untruths,
untruths that once ruled us, you and me,
all of us, and we jointly destroyed these.
Now untruths don't puzzle us, nor these
suffocate us.
Unimpaired emptying of visionless notions
strengthens us, our clashing notions jar us
no longer, it keeps us alive.
What is that that floors us on that

timeless, spaceless vibration?
Is it going to consume us?
Is it going to devour us?
You know not that.
So do I.

19

Gazing upon the flames of antiquated
layers of stranded thoughts,
I asked the angels,
"What does the stillness of innumerable daybreaks
have to proffer to us?"
Fumbling and stumbling,
the angels yelled at me,
"Why the hell are you digging our past?"
I whispered,
"Because in your past I see panic waving,
and men and women waning,
men and women fleeing
and history heaving."
And when the angels told me,
"You speak a language none of your generation does,
we have no answers",
the stars with their dream-dimmed eyes,
waited avidly for the sun to rise to gulp them.

20

What is profane and what is not?
To know that I entered beneath
the somber regimen of ethereal
thoughts,
that I, discreetly, clung to, randomly,
in order to tread the chosen inroads,
where I came across the vacant
visage of countless, unknown dreams
trying to disillusion the illusory

innocence.
"Of what?"
Purred this question someone into my ears.
"Of innocence of unreal masked visages."
I did purr, too.
Ruptured feelings, entangled, gave me a sense of
somnolence of nothingness moving slowly
into oblivion.
Synonymous with the requirements of universe,
we, part of connected segments,
move ahead.

21

Now, the images change and these change
dialogistically,
the images, too uncombed, too disheveled
and too uncultivated
reveal their confusion generously.
Sightless ideas chase me, incessantly,
and I swarm into field of truceless
contemplations,
stranded
in a master-slave relationship.
Elations of being a master and lord lording
over subsided abdications make you proud
but of what use is it to have
been starred with puny medals.
Elations like angst, more often than not,
don't erect properly.

22

"Immutable happenings are inevitable truths",
the moon that came too near to me, almost
within my reach, told me when I was on the
verge of being inflamed.
Parched hands took me into their lap

and having moiled me significantly
assured me of that immanent order for
which we exist, for ever.
Ambivalence of values
or
valueless ambivalence
ardently inspires me to whisper with
fading desolation.
I dared
and
I acted like a befuddled paranoid.

23

My voyage is relentlessly curly
and ruthlessly hoary.
Unlit lamp is sleeping now.
I shed myself behind the withdrawn
rays of light peeping shyly through
forbidden blanks.
Am I not trapped in a ceaseless continuum
of incessant flow?
Am I discovering myself?
Or
Am I entangled in dreadfully defenseless
obsessions,
dwindling, here and there
and shaking nothingness nowhere?

24

Coupled with unfriendly welcome,
the gestures lose their identity,
individually and collectively too.
They tell us:
The identities are undecipherable,
these are concealed long back by
the warbling liquids flowing in our minds.

These gestures would never encapsulate
the unconquerable corners of our mind,
for infirmities of our mind do hold us
together as we proceed to look at each other.
Some wordless meanings have crept into
our existence,
but these don't threaten us,
these hold us together.
To hell with you, we yowl, we, victims of nothingness
that oppresses.

25

That meaningless figure surges his head again,
unmindful of the presence of his peers.
None feels surprised.
Now-a-days meaningless figures don't surprise us.
Recent stories contain valueless premises of such
men.
These stories don't have that dreamy essence
of virtually everything that draws a line, a thin line
between divinity of creation and created divinity.
Primitive manifestations make me suffer the
disfigurements,
the grinning masks have their way, courtesy,
my serene silence.
No use in flinging my illumined thoughts behind,
none would respond.
This is what we call,
history on descent.

26

On that dilapidated debris lies a zombie.
That meaningless figure once ruled us, for long.
He ruled us more intellectually than
morally.
His shadows were in collusion,

his eyelashes never dwindled.
He never talked to us,
he never felt one with us.
Still we loved him,
for we loved interacting with zombie.
That meaningless figure had a riveting gaze that
never dislocated us.
We welcomed that gaze, for we were
blind,
our blindness was blissfully bright.
The zombie is now a corpse,
but we zombies treat that zombie as our master
and welcome,
"Is coming! Is coming!! Is coming!!!
All heartily welcome."[6]

27

In minds, pure and whimsical,
In minds, impure and sane,
fatigued inertia, accumulated inertia of
all generations, does dissect the agonizing
crevices of every moment we go through
to reach the threshold of our past.
Past is ugly.
Past is suffocating.
Past is melodious.
Past is grieving.
Our past does not resonate.
It is dead and thus it oppresses.

28

I do look forward to meet those
who have instilled insensibilities into

---

[6] Remember the lines James Joyce mentions in *Ulysses* in the context of Elijah's coming.

restlessness of mine,
restlessness as infecund as I am.
A scene occurs.
Men and their frozen lips give me
their fleeting glimpse.
Their fury is as cold as a century old
corpse in search of his lost soul.
My memories grow violent and
I go berserk.
I seek refuse in the subterranean edges
and am greeted by the same men and the
same frozen lips,
more agile than ever.

29

Infant immaturities loaf around openly
as if conspiratorial dreams of yesterdays
would be the thought provoking realities
of today.
Nothing can crush these.
We mortals have made these immortal.
I am a dissident now,
for, I have decided to surrender me to myself.
My fear is my biggest strength now,
for, I have learnt now how not to lead a
subdued existence.
I refuse to be a prisoner of my own yoke.
I refuse to believe in their invincibility.
I know what I am.
Zombies don't awe me now.
Life has ultimately dawned on me.

30

Deathless time walks on as circumspectly
as ever,
the cosmos lies naked before it struggling

to save itself from time's merciless surmises.
Lulling pangs of unwearied, formless stirrings
do visit us intermittently reminding us of
how inviolable our voices have become
and how invaluable we have become to time
and it's antics.
Our faith is shaking.
We have no faith in ourselves.
There is none who can redeem us now.
There is no elixir on this earth.
We are all unlidded.
We need a virgin.
To tame us.
Or leave us untamed.

31

That unwilling dispenser of justice
wakes up and then stepping out of himself
looks into imagined segments of unformed
life, wrapped in eroding layers.
"You don't use your hands magnanimously;
we are dying here and you relax there.
Is it what you are meant for?"
That recalcitrant child, already swallowed by
his defiling smallness, poses a teaser.
Before the reply could come,
unpurged oddities commence rationalizing
scattered remains of emptiness.
His destiny remains savagely impalpable,
he hardly bothers about it.

32

I hear a voice, a shrilling voice,
it speaks of unspeakable agony,
it has lorded over till time
immemorial.

The voice exults.
The voice invades me.
Inscrutability and impenetrability
of the voice burn me from within.
I shudder at my guileless infatuation
with the voice,
for, interruptions don't stop the invasion,
now that continuity of history is
no problem to us.

33

In the synod of souls, they ask,
"Can it last any longer?
Can burden of carrying wile memories
last any longer?"
Perhaps not.
I delved into fathomless riddles
that have held me to ransom for too long.
I am not afraid of those quirky souls
hanging fire wantonly.
The souls are crippling.
None would anchor these souls.
These souls cease to enchant me.
My fairyland that I have fancied about
since my childhood has tiptoed me
compromisingly as if I don't deserve it.
Tell me, then,
"Have the souls not killed my fairyland?"

34

Outlines become more and more tepid.
A sense of nothingness crowds it
and crowds it elegantly.
Some day these outlines would be writing myths
and would be expecting me to kneel down.
The language of the myths I don't understand,

for, I hail from the land where people are fed on
muddling myths.
The unease rustles.
The glimpses collude.
Dullness revels in veils of reverence.
And I look forward to meeting the true story
amidst longings for languid hopes and lingering
discourses.

35

This is a world in a state of stupor
bereft of love and ambition
and full of faithless faiths.
Farcically self-seeking nymphs
recall from their shrinking memory
stories of dismantled wishes, unfulfilled.
I don't wish to hear these stories,
my ears are completely extinguished,
exhausted.
My respect for you storytellers is
shaking my love for myself.
You cannot claw at me,
I have enlivened myself again.
I welcome erasures
that wipe out traces
of historical impotency.
So writ large.

36

The sounds of crusting lust for things
come to us in steely interruptions.
We, often, go berserk,
hysterical, paranoid, manic,
tyrannical.
Knowing not why.
Without thinking and

without mental pain and
without ecstatic sense of grief.
This is not a new apprehension,
we are too well trained in this art,
mental pain subjugates our faculties,
our faculties have refined curves
we have so wantonly nurtured.

37

Our failures, all encompassing,
our failures, eerily arranged,
we don't look at them,
we are too tired of ourselves,
we know how liquefying we are, for we know
"Reason is madness."[7]
Our intentions have fluid meanings,
our dipping thoughts hold us,
all of us together,
we wait for our end,
an unripe end.
And in that end,
all of us rejoice at
the beginning of a new beginning.

38

You are blotted out,
all of us seek light,
all of us know our dullness,
all are caught in a blind ally.
We cannot foresee what would happen
next moment,
we can only insinuate those we
fear to interact with,
we can see our identities in

[7] Edgar in *King Lear* (Act IV/Scene VI).

monstrous mirrors.
We enjoy our intrinsic desires no longer,
we bed comfortably with our elemental
passions.
Someday our victories would become
our defeats,
we would then realize how congealed our
blood has become,
we would be lost in the quagmire of
inconsequential intangibilities.
We love mute and dumb symbols.

39

The gulf accentuates,
here and far afield.
Idle questions fill the gulf.
Potentialities are becoming infinitely
conflicting.
I fail to discipline my emotions.
My emotions are too sterile.
Amorphous remorse paralyses me.
Severity of bidding adieu and harshness of togetherness
come together inhibiting the beguiling gulf.
The gulf is my dwelling place.
I seek solace in it.
I get it by making my emotions more sterile.
And towards the gulf's end
shapeless awareness of futile existence speaks of itself:
"My Destiny! Droll thing life is—that mysterious
arrangement
of merciless logic for a futile purpose!"[8]
Oppressiveness of nothingness;
circle completed.
Many sub-circles, staying incomplete.

---

[8] Joseph Conrad in *Heart Of Darkness.*

Cicada And Harlot

Night, a great visionary,
Life, an abstract entity and obliging,
You alive, giving hope to ensuing morning.

The hazy warmth of her lips,
Too engaging, too enchanting,
I, lost, on the borders of my desires.

Her unlit embracement,
Too cozy, too improvising,
You active, mired in your echoing lullabies.

Elements seek reconciliation,
As we hug each other,
I, sinking deep, down...and down...?

Celestial debauchery,
Falling in mutilated fragments,
You, in everlasting hurry to see the end.

A dark and insane empire,
You lord over,
That harlot bids me adieu, silently.

In morning, I lose everything,
Her, you, myself, everything,
And then wait insolently for yet another night.

Vexations

I don't venerate depths now,
I have overcome my inertia.
That enigmatic object fascinates
me no longer,
I have avenged my amnesia.
That enkindling entity sates me
perfectly, for that entity never
overpowers me.
Misconceptions do hunt me no longer,
incessant clash inspires me.
The glimmer of the moment condenses;
what remains stays with me.
The hours have become empty,
I don't ask them to fill themselves.
Now, days are not languorous any longer,
These are unfilled: whole, incomplete.
Though, I have many Lucifers, too many
Of them;
Still, they never make me feel deprived of
"joys of heaven".[1]
And I seek panacea in tumultuous vexations.

[1] "No, Faustus, curse thyself. Curse Lucifer, That hath deprived thee of the joys of heaven." Towards the end, nemesis visits upon Dr Faustus in Marlowe's *Dr Faustus*. (5.2)

Mother

She confesses it to me,
as to many others,
she wants to die,
she has lived too long,
she feels one with death,
life has never come to her
alive.
She has ceased to suffer
pain,
she has refused to defer
her pains,
she has learnt she can have
no world of her own.
When the world sleeps,
she stays awake, weeps,
she waits for the angel,
the errorless angel,
from sky,
who has hidden himself in
the clouds peppering the sky.
She has a long, painful stare
bringing her a nasty hopelessness
and scary helplessness.
Umpteen times,
umpteen times,
I have heard this story from her,
knobbly,
I am fed up now,
I tell her,
umpteen times,
umpteen times,

there is no angel,
the world never sleeps,
none has a separate world,
our stares don't mean anything,
these are mummified stares,
life is dead for all of us.
She laughs,
and tells me,
too young to know what life is all about,
life is a streak of madness,
it absorbs all insanities under the sun
and that rarity of sanity is what she waits for,
she waits for the virtues people have forged,
she waits for that angel that has blinded her to
the enigmas of her day-dreaming,
she waits for the eyes that would give her new hopes,
she has lived so long waiting for all these and
many more,
it has been a wait in a lurch, she knows.
And never, never, she says it,
"O dark, dark, dark, amid the blaze of noon,
Irrecoverably dark, total eclipse
Without all hope of day!"[1]
She waits...waits...waits.
She kisses me.
I feel the kiss has numbed me.
She embraces me.
I feel the embracement has aroused a passion
I have allayed so far.
She elasticizes me and tells me to sleep.
I sleep. I get up.
I find her sleeping,
for good.
She is dead,

[1] Milton in *Samson Agonistes.*

having lived an answerless life
and with her are dead
the angel,
the stares,
the pains,
the day-dreaming.

Thy Face; Great Anarch

(For that enigmatic one: one I met last a decade back or even much earlier; parting words do l...i...n...g...e...r...in my memory; relations neither forgotten nor lost, most revered relations. If, someday, ever read this poem; my words don't ring false, believe these.)

Part I

And that emerging beauty,
that perishing beauty, that perishing age,
beauty pieces together the hopes, incontinent hopes,
dismounted through senseless efforts.

No two similar things do exist in this world,
In you only, I felt,

"...scent was musk and...cheek was rose;
...teeth are pearls and...lips drop wine;
...form is a brand and...hips a hill;
...hair is night and...face moonshine."[1]

And, again,

"...cheeks so rare a white was on,
No daisy makes comparison,
(Who sees them is undone),
For streaks of red were mingled there,

...lips were red, and one was thin,
Compar'd to that was next her chin,
(Some bee had strung it newly);[2]

---

1 Extracts from the story told on twenty-first night in *Tales From 1001 Arabian Nights*. Those who have read this story might say: comparisons are odious.

2 Sir John Suckling, a Cavalier poet in *A Ballad Upon A Wedding*.

You make my memory
the greatest tyrant for me,
atrociously stirring it up, off and on,
and I find myself unwinding in a swathe
of gloam, velvety,
not far away from me.

I have seen things
over a stretched period of time,
nothing but only that stays
with that tyrant,
blithe, flashing up and dieing away
(rapidly and repeatedly)
embryonic,
restlessly falsifying, disgustingly
beguiling and mischievously tranquilizing.
Thy face, great anarch.

Thy face,
layers of beauty;
freshly fallen snow,
freezing the apostles and
the prophets alike.

Thalia,
Aglaia,
Eupherosyne.[3]

Thy glittering face foists upon me dazzling
endowments of desires,
magnanimously,
inspiring ecstasies to crowd
the aligned corners of my mind
and I add fiercely to the tyranny of my memory
flames of innocence.

---

[3] The three Graces i.e. beauty, gentleness and grace in Greek mythology.

The images never recede,
the fantasies, brought to the fore, never
rapture,
the softness never contrives,
the kindred fragrance never
unravels.
Thy face, great anarch.

Searching redrawn contours,
cased in linear firmaments,
I frighteningly borrow from thy seductive face
my own meandering.

Searching unexplored possibilities within
unexploited desert of uniqueness
I surreptitiously steel from thy face,
the explored possibilities
I fascinate myself with.

That sparkling adornment of thy
anarchy,
have I not carried too far?

Thy anarchy feigns a fairer and slier
dross,
the cauldron of my memory, helpless,
you re-sprout and re-sprout yourself,
instantaneously,
springing the lines I pen.

Sparkling blushes i.e. my hopes,
the sojourners,
pep up inclinations,
imaginative speculations,
and I pen these lines now.
Ten years later.

Neither truths nor untruths,
Neither finites nor infinities,
Neither pleasures nor pains,
Neither beginnings nor ends,
Nothing fades thy beauty.
Alas?
Beauty carries its own pain.
I bear it.

Part II

You, a resplendent wind,
sparkling and alive in everything
taking me into your lap, lulling
me into deepening sleep,
motionless.

You, a melting fire,
numbing the impulses within me
tempting me to enthrall myself
amid the pains of obscured
association.

You, a blazing sapphire,
standing still, applauding sagaciously
my memories, that while unearthing
I thought would neither fade away
nor wither away.

You, a scintilating shore,
wiping out the captive thoughts I
had chosen, meticulously for the
memoirs I would be marveling into
while being in suffocating solitude.

You, a mesmerizing suave,
queering the traces of momentariness,
I so exquisitely believed, would remain

with me mitigating the discomforts of my
frail sorrow.

You, a despairing hope,
tremulously calming the oddities of
unfathomable bliss that I thought
would compensate for the exalted dreams,
severed from the realities.

You, a guileless treasure,
beguiling the naiveties of wanton
desires that I thought would sleep with
me on those beds of dreamless dreams
where alienness reigned supreme.

You, a stirring thought,
worming your way through the
stymied layers of my unknowable
mind where calmly rested the
conspicuousness of your presence.

You, a shrimped time,
fleeting, fleeting and fleeting
leaving me with the time's glint
of uncontrollable absurdities,
my very own creation.

You, an infinite inspiration,
transgressing the boundaries of the
mind wherein lay unclad the
countervailing reminiscences of
retrieved past, dwindling.
All this praise, you deserve, as
"Such praise is yours—and such shall you possess,"[4]
In the memoirs and in the dreams,
in the illusions and in the

---

[4] Alexander Pope in *To Belinda*.

hallucinations, in the morbidities
of imaginative quietude and in the
subdued beam of fading hope,
I keep staying, unmindful of who
you are.

Part III

You came to me

(a)

through the vacuums
and their surroundings, through the
loneliness and its grips when I
longed for you,

(b)

through the stirrings,
the usurpations of my lumpish,
infallible, confessions that I made to
you when you abhorred me,

(c)

through the enigmas, the errorless foundations
I thought of you when you
uninitiated me into your beguiling being,

(d)

through the calm
grandeur of restlessness coming
my way when ardours of my longing
for you ceased suddenly,

(e)

through the glories,
the sprouting and re-sprouting

of trysts I made unknowingly
with mists of forgotten memoirs,

(f)

through the melancholic
moods when you frequented there,
exhuming the low vitalities equalizing
the tranquilized ebbs and the flows,

(g)

through the enraptured
eccentricities of passion and aversion,
you obscured, piously, my sanity
and befuddled, impiously, my insanity,

(h)

through the derisive fantasies
about unseen past and unmet future
where you besieged me in a dream world
with your entreasured pleasures,

(i)

through the descending heights,
raved images that I borrowed
from you when you mingled your sadness
with blooming innocence,

(j)

through the ascending depths,
the dwindling traces, you
lent me majestically enkindling the recesses
of never awakened wishes,

(k)

through the wavering, tall trees,
peeping inside the windows, whispering to

me sagaciously about the fruitlessness of my
long, arduous wait for you,

(l)

through the realms of niggardly
glares you nonchalantly threw at me, ignoring
the chaotic despairs that would follow suit,

(m)

through the dreams wherein
I unearthed heavenly acquired equanimities,
skillfully grafted in you,

(n)

through the scattered wishes
crowding numerous corners of my mind,

(o)

through my clambering of the unreal roads,
you had already blocked,

(p)

through the unformed contours
I came across throughout when I was with myself and
also when I was not, for it was my
soliloquy that wiped out the thin demarcation
between whether you are or you are not.

I know the age of today triumphs over
the age of yesterday, but now, I imagine,
the world, "hast a lady for more beautiful
Than any woman in this waning age."[5]
I miss you.

---

[5] Shakespeare in *The Taming Of The Shrew*. Induction—Scene II.

Allusions

Rains descended from the heaven,
and drenched her to her core.
Having thought, for a while,
over the matters ponderous,
I felt what dryness was all about.

Exclusiveness in its ubiquity fell
from everywhere,
and absorbed her florid quietness, mutely.
Having thought, for a while,
over the dulled trivialities,
I felt what depth of innocence was all about.

Bright and shining images recoiled
innocently,
and wrecked the ruins around her.
In the infinitude of my own mortifications,
I could feel voiceless voices voicing something.

I wouldn't quiz her about her choicest
ecstasies,
and also about her substance.
Nor would I quiz her about the remnants of
her musical humility
and its morbid stillness.

Allusions do have their limitations,
these fly, endlessly,
demurred and obstinated.

Lightly engrossed in elevated incongruities,
I severed their (allusions) internal relationships.

I looked through these allusions,
my intellectual restraints loathed my narrowness.
And her eyes gave a pensive look to the triumphal
sensuality of my stilted mind.

The glass has just broken.
Scattered and scattered.
I heard no echo.

She peeped into broken glasses,
castigating me for not seeing
the allusions,
tamed me there, for a while,
and I saw no reason why should I leave
the allusions.

Can an echo represent an allusion?
Can separation represent togetherness?
Can what is not lost represent the gain?
Can turbulence represent concealed peace?

Old Man And His Conflicts

I, an old man now, too old and too obsolete,
look at the broken alliances of my tasteless
youth and decayed sense of associations,
of which I thought, in my heyday, as
intensifying, integrating ascetic indignities.
Now the musical frivolities of my childhood
don't even purr near me,
running amuck as people on seeing
a mad elephant going berserk.
My senses are in delirium, fascinated
by their youthful adversaries,
and I beautifully hallucinated by the fantasies
I forgot, in my heyday, to juxtapose with
heuristic, scintillating realities.
Her betrayals, I remember now, wore
the garb of contemptuous calumny,
the moon was so silent, that day,
perhaps pondering over the absurdities of fate.
On the verge of despair, once I sought a quite
habitation.
What was wrong with it?

Perhaps everything came out of everything
else.
Too puzzling and too perplexing.
So do I console myself now?
My apprehensions were too sensuous, then,
too superficial.
Alas, their heroic deeds don't enchant me now.
I see now where significance submerges into
insignificance and *vice versa.*

All my past days are sealed, now.
I can't break these open.
Fate has many such discretions.
The inner side of everything I had, then, was bright,
the inner side of nothing I didn't have was murky.
Everything was formless.
Nothing was shapeless.
The disbelief, almost complete now is mythical and mystical.
Did it not clamber away when it was most welcome?

Crumbling away, far off, the initial symbols of my end
knock at my door, sanely, warning me I
should not sway away with anything
around me.
Should I hear?
Like a restless eagle, I stare at the opalescent blanks
that expand near me, warning me not to walk
ceaselessly around my unmet expressions.
Should I hear?
Should I slip into obvious, unwelcome?
Or should I embrace it?
I walk alone on my path,
towards my death,
with pride, my hand raised.

Fading Roots Of Childhood

Through the threshold of childhood,
I limped towards the miracles of youth.
On the horizon, passive but firm, saw I
the eclipsing glimpses of worn out
roots.
The smoggy,
seizing of the facts,
the realities
of tales of falsehood, so cherished,
advance.

Scars don't heal suddenly,
Scars are not out of hiding.
As yet.

I walk with my unsavory movements,
someone halts me, reminding
me of the ultimate festivals of atonement,
one has to pursue, sometimes for long,
to reach.
Swollen I stand, aghast,
joyously leaping youth,
looks forward to meeting
the incredulous motives.
Stories lie in silhouetted remembrances
circling faded roots.

The menacing miseries don't heal suddenly.
The soliloquy of the silent is not out of hiding.
As yet.

Wipe out,
grapple with,

the crumbling traces of childhood,
the smokes of cynical traces,
youth is just an outpost.
Sensuous perceptions bemoan the arrival
of the images we wrongly believe are
left in the burial grounds,
barren for long.

The roots that are timidly talked of
by persons, renowned,
enshrine themselves in a vacuum of
crystallized infatuations.
Alive for so long.
undeterred, the fading roots hop around,
majestically, in a state of softened tranquility,
as if the wiliness in us,
on the verge of its
own arrival.

Wretched lingering of rootless
dilemmas contain me conceitedly,
force me to disown my
own sagacity.
Too ignominious indeed.

Disintegrated Self

Attachment to self.
Detachment from self.
And growing between them,
indifference.
T.S. Eliot completes his three conditions,
conditions looking alike yet differing completely,
flourishing "in the same hedgerow".[1]

Our self, the self we, you and I have.
Don't we, at times, get afraid of the shadows
of the self we cower in?
We now have allowed, majestically,
the shadows to choke the true self, our
very own, to
stay unbridled, in that murky
prominence.

Within its exteriority, the self searches aimlessly
the consolations, the contours of questions
it nonchalantly negated in its self-revelation.
You have intellectual emptiness,
ruthlessly muffling the consoling cobwebs,
symbolic of unmet interiors.

Jaded self walks with reveries of escape towards
pyramids standing firm, queering the uprooted,
self-controlled concealments.
Don't fear.
Go to the instantaneous frames of our sagging memory.
Futile alienation, awfully busy.

---

[1] *Little Gidding* by T.S. Eliot.

This oasis of perfect self where we look at the
definition of logics of illogical judgments, has
started seeking extraordinary pleasures
in drooping, known unrealities.

Uprush of what we are never comfortable with
and what we have never been uncomfortable with
come galore,
our morbidities are self-swinging
between the limits we neither defined nor redefined.

Doddering within us is the desire and
its unrecognizable destructiveness.
Self-choosing to dissolve into it.
What lords over what?

Inconspicuous subterranean turmoil, all over, smiles,
peevishly, at the anguish of psychic contents,
their residues, disintegrating our
whole self, leaving us in ecstasy
of a veiled lurch.

Through an array of unarranged questions,
history has adjudged, as part of incoherent deliria,
the ebbs and the flows
we measure with our massy self, disjunctively.

Self relaxes amid fetishistic enthrallment of
the relaxing anxieties,
we with our imprisoned self look into
the meanings in the captive arenas, we
once determined for the survival of our self.

Your strife is not hidden;
emanating from
the clotted boundaries the self never enters.
Still, you don't talk of it.

We prefer to sit by the window of our self and
stare in the dark, unable to make out:
"Which is worse: The dark inside, or the darkness out."[2]

?...?
inimical,
inimical to the self, that has been so
unfaithful, so traumatizing to us
strives alone,
distracting us all from what we have tackled
all along.

Whose shadows are we trying to trace in ?...?
In order to get our true self back.

The homeless question continues.

[2] Joseph Brodsky in *I Sit by the Window*. (translated by Howard Moss)

Vespers Of Life

Substantial things of life I sought
when I was perilously wasted,
and these came to me in plethoric
numbers, incredulously.
Plunging deep into the paradigm
of rattling, headless shadows,
I fought, helplessly, those dreary
arrivals of sad and melancholic
passions, hidden, beneath
the façade,
these superior things wrapped
themselves in.

Substantial things of life I sought
when I was fabulously peaked,
and these came to me scarcely
in monotonic absurdities.
I plunged deep into the quietude
of dignified darkness, gemmed with
static imageries which toyed
shamelessly with these substantial things
that lay there unclad.

But could anyone of the two stop
me from being hitch-hiked to
the vespers of life that
deluded me into catching the
soundless flux of vespers?

Posterity yet to decree its verdict.

Confusions

Oftentimes,
frequented by our fluorescent inquest,
stealthily,
we rush around the boundaries; countless boundaries,
seemingly erect
like fearless monsters.

To these boundaries,
we go with our questions,
questions about distinctions,
between

realities and obsessions,
individual sanities and collective insanities,
joyful pains and joyless pleasures
numbing anxieties and betraying fears,

swirling whispers and blissful activities
ailing dreams and fossilizing realities,
melodic eccentricities and unmelodic sobrieties
exotic imageries and rebelling
fantasies,

adorned illusions and unadorned hallucinations
moronic desires and unfeigned wisdom,
rationality of intuitions and irrationality of inquisitions
enthralling fascinations and disenthralling anguishes,

dwarfed ignoramuses and gigantic ignominies
inherited sophistries and acquired conceits,
weirdly guarded greatness and fictitiously displayed
goodness,
colossal disparities and incalculable reactions,

perilous debasements and plenteous reinforcements,
self-punishing immunities and
self-dissipating oddities,

artistic beauty and inartistic grandeur
wondrous symmetries and marvelous
asymmetries,

exalted implicitness and exhumed explicitness
sonorous obscurities and edified
apocalypse.

We keep orbiting
around these questions,
these boundaries,
and a faint, genteel vision comes to our
rescue,
we cling on to that and complete our sojourn,
our odyssey: our life.

Grotesque Masks

We crawl slowly into the wilderness of
their jejunely insipid perfections,
earnestly hoping to confront them with
their
(their or of jejunely insipid?)
irreversibility.
Figure submerging into background.

Immensely pleased, they strut to and fro
in an aquarium, tiny,
insensibly joyous,
cheery faces carry
(their or of sunken imperfections?)
the load of
their sunken imperfections.
Background overshadowing figures.

Their exquisite paleness, writ large,
everywhere,
wondrous rigidities of their
(their or of intellectual apogee?)
intellectual apogee, in deeds and in
misdeeds alike.
Figures lulling background
or *vice versa*.

The masks,
crowned on triumphal chariot,
and
we whimper,
at
their protozoic grotesqueness.

Broken Time

Broken time has no refined frames,
obvious form, unmeasured contents;
nothing of it frozen in historical frames.
Broken time; no resurrection of
withered eventualities.
Broken time has no eyes of its own,
introspecting eyes.
These eyes, sleepless eyes;
not born blind.
Alas! these have gone for penance,
multiple penance.
For good.
Who, then, trod it?
And who now tread it?

Broken time,
it's shrinking shadows in the gaps,
it's languishing sound in
the gaps,
it's own eternal images in the gaps
it's zigzagging, pimpled beauty in the gaps,
it's hues in the gaps,
it's exuberance in the gaps,
it's emblems of piousness,
it's visageless sound in the gaps,
it's flirtatiousness in the gaps,
it's inkiness in the gaps.

Broken time swells.
Broken time dwells.
Broken time blows.
Broken time glows.

Broken time whirls.
Broken time twirls.

Surging, surging, surging and thus surges
the broken time.
From a frameless history?
Or from the endless cosmos?
Or from a hibernating consciousness and
what lies beneath that?
Or from the chaotic, never evaporating unconsciousness
and what bares that?
Or from the orbit of time with its sprawling edges?

Don't talk of our dreams.
Broken time drives our dreams to its own land.
Our dreams search a land of their own, for,
our dreams are such as none can vie with,
our dreams are such as none can clash with,
our dreams are such as none can cope with.
Our dreams search a land of their own, for,
the planet, the present one is too short for
the dreams,
the inhuman dimensions do unsettle the
human dimensions,
the littleness of our existence overshadows
the prodigious ingenuity, inherited,
our realities are too impotent to even
associate with our dreams.

BLURED DREAMS.
DREAMS BLURED.
BOTH BEREFT OF
STILTED REALITIES.
REALITIES IN ANGUISH.
DREAMS GUARD.
DREAMS AWAKEN.

REALITIES IN THEIR GRAVEYARDS.

Broken time ensues the time that continues,
continues and continues.
Time continues and what remains there
in the chalice,
the chalice of broken time;
unalterable moments of history.
Which determinates which?
History making time or time making
history is indeterminable,
terminably as indeterminable and
interminably as determinable as
what lie unclad in the cauldron
of broken time.

Oh! That One Year Get-together And Our Very Own, Mr Monsieur Maillard[1]

1

I, The Split-Speaker

What a lofty thought today I have!
"I should split my psyche,
methinks, I must visit my days,
when they and I were supposed
to be formed for the decades to come."
That cold, wintry afternoon, and those
cold icy thoughts trickling down my spine,
a place bringing to the fore the beauty
out of creatures, live and agile,
out of trees, tall and green,
out of smoky evening, glaring, nearby.
The roads were full,
activities on the move,
beautiful girls strolling, handsome boys
whispering,
snow was calm, composed,
the tossed laughter of that girl,
a passer by,
remains a pain for me.
Pains are the things one can live by,
not the unkindness.
I enjoy the pain of being a human being the most.
And now my memory compels me to come to that
narrow lane, opening with a heap of garbage

---

1 A Principal character in Edgar Allan Poe's story 'The System Of Doctor Tarr And Professor Fether'.

and a public lavatory,
a lane I would be passing, to and fro,
umpteen times, a month.
The serenity around lures me, allures me.
"Am I in St Petersberg? Dostoevsky[2] and his St Petersburg.
Hellish congestion. Now when congestion has come,
can Dostoevsky's characters be far behind?"
I did buttonhole myself.
Was my fear displaced?
Or was I misplaced?

2

The Initiation

8 P.M.
That big lounge, so many chaps there,
young boys or men, young girls or women,
attired beautifully.
Utter confusion prevailing,
all doing the same thing simultaneously,
talking, giggling, laughing, teasing,
smiling, gossiping and smoking.
That ogler ogled.
The jeering ladies doing wonders with
their possessions.
The whining gentlemen doing wonders with
their disguise.
Verging on despair,
they knew not what discrepancies in their heart,
their brain, their unconscious mind were all about.
A chaotic noise, a chaotic congestion.
Pippa Passes proved so wrong on this earth.

---

[2] St Petersburg is the locale in Dostoevsky's important novels like *The Idiot, Crime And Punishment* etc. It is important to understand the linkages the writer develops between the place, the chaotic and confused life his characters lead and the problem of conscience.

"God's in His heaven—
All's right with the world!"[3]
The world in that big hall was shaking,
towering persons ruling the roost.
Frenzied gathering of frenzied persons
behaving as if all of them were the
gospel truths.
For instance,
that bulky, moustached man flew his kiss,
as if his hands were snake, his lips hissing.
"Hi, Hi, Hi, Hi..."
that short, thin, bearded chap uttering
nonchalantly.
An anglicized gentleman.
An Indian.
I guess so.
Idealess young men, idling young women
had come together,
to pen one of the chequered chapters of their history.
Twelve at night.
I see their plight.
We, on the path of glowing dim.

3

Mummery and Mumchance

Absurdly noisy nights.
Uncertainties yawning.
Unfinished spaces asking for more.
"Where should I retreat?
Everything around
as hollow as that bulky, moustached man's
flying kiss."
Congestion, I treading on their
stillness.

---

[3] Robert Browning in PIPPA PASSES.

That tiny mirror, on the wall, and my face in it,
I read various meanings into my face,
for the first time, I saw meanings in my face.
I had my early lessons,
faces could have multitudinous meanings,
all conflicting, all suffocating, all crawling.
"Nothing here would prompt my mind. I have come
to a place that wouldn't prompt anything."
I, a mumchance, reassured myself when that curly-lipped
girl came out of the sports' room,
with a nasal voice.
Her voice, strange, baritone,
bemused me.

4
Dawn Breaks Out

"Good, good", someone cried,
from inside the dining hall,
loud voice and a louder laughter,
the short, thin, bearded, the anglicized
chap entering the hall, adding his laughter
to that voice.
Inside life had started searching itself.
The blizzard last night had left
young cheeks, younger and rosier.
The moustached, bulky fellow felt cozier.
Everyone was doing the same thing.
talking, giggling, gossiping, planning,
the ogler kept ogling.
The excitement knew no bounds.
I had landed in a place, a place
where "Though cockcrow marches crying of false dawns
Shall bury my dark voice, yet still it mourns,
Among the ruins....[4]

---

[4] Edith Sitwell in *The Little Ghost Who Died For Love.*

Groups, in the making,
Identities, submerging,
Equations, getting evolved,
I, on my way to greater catastrophe.

5

Those Big, Ejaculating Eyes

Those large, big, hungry, eyes,
thin at the top,
the possessor of those eyes and that
balding head passed by.
No glances around.
Rogue feelings conveyed,
he meant business.
It was willed that he would ruin us,
water had started getting muddled
into the room of the meddler as I ushered.
I stood in an aura of offending arrogance.
A look, hard, nasty and ridiculous
came my way and a castigation flew
from his loud mouth,
"You from cow belt. You must know
how to talk. I have twenty-five years of experience"
On my leaving the room, someone, inside me, purred
into my ears,
"You ought to pay the price
for your birth, your isolated life. You are unfit here."

6

The God/Goddess Of Sex, Intrigue, Rising Libido/High Performers

Sex, thou has so many forms.
Those high performers,
anarchy of their actions and
the reactions,

The mourner and
the mourned,
surreal images of vanishing
deeds and ravishing misdeeds.
Sex annihilates the relations,
it annihilates the longings,
symbolizing delusional illusion,
disharmonizing clubbed harmonies,
prospering inside the shattered dreams
young men,
women cultivated.
Sex has an elusive quality,
it walks on and on and on
and fails to bring to the fore the inexplicable behavior
we are ashamed of.
Sex is the greatest intriguer,
conspiring against the conspirators,
conspirators competing with each other,
visible yielding place to invisible.

7

St. Vitus' Dance[5]/31st December

"How would you celebrate? An important occasion."
asked, the fellow, his eyes ejaculating,
expecting an answer suiting his needs.
"Hee…hee...hee…heeee…."
giggled that lady whose wont it was to mouth,
"Hee...heee…hee…heeee"
"Yeah, yeah we must, we must. Bonfire, drinks,
dance…", the moustached man uttered loudly,
his eyes twinkling.

---

[5] Also known as "tarantism", St Vitus' dance implies mass madness where people are affected by dance manias that involve dancing. raving, convulsions etc. These epidemics were noticed most frequently in fifteenth and sixteenth century.

"Heee...heeeee...heeeeeee."
That large-eyed gentleman and that ejaculating look,
Good Heavens, he penetrated so many
though his eyes.
In retrospect, tell me, did anyone of them deserve
a look, I asked my friend, very thin, very tall, years later,
laughed he, jerking his head,
"If wishes were horses, beggars would ride,
frustrated bastards."

8

It Ultimately Started

The clock, an old, rusty clock stroke twelve.
And hay-presto,
you have that large-eyed chap entering from
the ladies door,
taking all but a few by complete surprise.
My friend having farted around in the congested hall
took me along, I, with trepidation, yelled,
"Whereto?"
Exotic scenes welcomed us,
that charmer of charmers, duly flanked by charming
ladies, fashionably attired,
jostled for space as the large-eyed chap entered the fray.
The ancient ages were on display,
St Vitus' dance,
dancers going haywire,
that short girl had a pray in sight.
The bazaar nosier and murkier.
Darkness at its zenith.
Seeds sown.

9

Flows An Uneasy Quietus

The days that follow the nights,
the nights that follow the days,

time ticking away and the uneasy
calm paving the way for bigger
disquietude, already on the anvil.
Gentlemen showing ungentlemanliness,
the fair lady becoming fairer, worse,
the dusky one duskier, worse,
and that great foxy chap smelt a rat.
All were frenzy-struck.
Hells breaking lose slowly.
A bitter mystery unfolding itself,
a lighter ghost overpowering us.
In between passion and precision,
the foxy chap, egged on, choose
none.

10

Alienations And Group Dynamics

Rapt gaze, that galoot, his lost invincibility,
the beast inside that galoot kept laughing,
his quizzing visage bright with villainy,
seeking pleasure in newer ideas, the group
never lacked.
Sky is the limit.
Immense possibilities.
Explore, explore.
Futile exercises holding all to ransom,
players around the dining table,
not thinking alike, behaved alike.
Outer shells intact.
Inner ones fragmented.
Life beginning with that table,
culminating into broken words,
being whispered aloud.
I queried where these meaningless words
would lead us.

11

Auto-Ironies

They talk of clear vision.
They must visit this place.
They must not fear being hurt,
there is no heart here, no soul here,
only stories are told,
by room bearers,
old, simple, peaky and weak,
room bearers, with no voice,
polish our shoes; we, Brown Saheb's shoes.
These stories bring to us glimpses
of our wretchedness, past of the place
is privy to,
these tell us of Brown Sahibs, of their
love, of their deserted beloveds,
of their forgotten promises,
of my loneliness, tiring and self-defiling.
It is a place I remember as replete with
auto-ironies,
and confusing culture,
faint, stultifying, coercive, idle.

12

d'edoublement Of Self

All of us faced a peculiar problem,
a problem of self-definition,
a problem of self-acquisition.
Everyone acted like a jeopardized rescuer
rescuing himself from self-intuition.
We didn't breathe any wish now,
we were a degenerated lot now,
we were totally lost in a heap of incoming infamy.
Our sterility, intransigent,
our egos, perilous reservoir of our conflicts.

And of our frustrations too.
Of our obsessions too.
Our self eluded self-scrutiny,
We, disharmoniously trapped
within our self-appeasing harmonies.
That feeling crawled within us,
underneath our naked falsehood.

13
Abstract Quiddities

In that crowd, motley crowd of thirty,
one lived only with oneself,
they never lived together,
togetherness was the curse,
those were the cursed years,
the years deprived of idealism, faith,
trust and joy.
Our assumptions had wrong foundations,
our presumptions had malignant deception,
we looked forward to meeting abstract
meanings in immediate circumstances
to live the life of orphaned children.
Our life there traveled fearfully
amidst the restlessness of our own
quiddities.
Strangely indifferent we were.

14
Obscure Odyssey

Time brought a gift for us,
the gift of saying adieu.
Depart we would as ordained.
Held captive for too long,
ruled for too long,
we, the subjugated fellows,
we stooped low, everywhere,

anytime.
The nightmare was over,
nightmarish vision overshadowed us.
We cannot glory in the years we spent together,
it was a life full of
vile ambitions and low achievements.
It was a life dissembled to the core.
We learnt how to make our utterances untruthful,
our initiation into maturity stigmatized,
our hopes filled with "gaudy shapes"[6]
we set off on an odyssey,
an unsure,
obscure odyssey.

15
Who Was Our Mr Monsieur Maillard?

Who, then, my friends, was our Mr Monsieur Maillard?
Who enraged a few of us?
Ponder over it.
Get back to me, if you can
Or go to the hell.
None cares,
Tell me what happed in the aftermath of
these years.
Must have been fructifying.
"Right you are. For a few, indeed. For the
rest, it has been unrest, almost."
I give my assessment.
Tell me,
Were we formed?
Or reformed?
Or deformed?
Who will answer these doubtings...?

---

[6] "And fancies fond with gaudy shapes possess..." Milton in IL PENSEROSO.

Perhaps, the walls,
we have walled ourselves;
and we have walled our incompleteness;
our deficiencies;
our idiosyncrasies;
these very walls, would, someday,
come walking to us,
and reveal the stories we have penned
ourselves.
Long back.

Rare Moments

Some moments come;
they pass,
still,
they haunt us, defenselessly,
for long,
crossing all limits
time places on us.

In our rejoice,
as in our mourning,
these moments blind us
from within;
making us strong,
holding our hopes firm
as if, our perfectly mirrored
hopes would have died
but for these moments.

Our most beauteous
remembrances
hang heavily on these
moments
but
on the abyss,
surrounding these moments,
would be our ugly ones too.

Still, sometimes, these
moments frighten us,
unrelentingly,
telling us
what walks into us,

surreptitiously,
through these moments
are dreams
to live by.

God And Beggar

That plain queerness angers me, chases me,
with its usual peripheries.
I, a beggar, refuse to own them,
for their sake,
their blurredness keeps wandering along,
for my sake.
Scattered faces look askance at me;
thinking I would collapse soon, like froth.
It has been a case of slow eclipse,
I am waiting for my queerness to unravel,
the reservoir of my eternal quietude is dried,
the aftermath of moments gone, grills at me.
My life is full of disjointedness,
from one that is dead is born the one that is
to die, soon.
The painter, we call God,
who has been painting for my
survival,
lives sagaciously on the divine lines
dazzled, at times, over the absurdities of
his painting.
I cannot peel the painter away in my
frozen togetherness with the painter.
I am consoled, I am consoled, consoled
by the queerness the painter has bequeathed me.
My consolation does drift away, slowly, shyly,
as the painter keeps painting,
within his enseamed divinity.

Imageries Or Dull Realities

Once upon a time, I was alone,
my solitude taking me to those
bygone pages of my youth
I shun falling upon again.
The youth had trifles of its own.
I thought of the trifles
and they did cling around me,
for, I was afraid of again dwelling along
the imageries,
unfaithful imageries.
I knew you, you, the radiant-eyed
girl,
aren't you the same?
You emerge from the mysterious circles;
entreating me not to forget you in my
dim-remembered imageries.
I tell you, you are beyond imageries,
you are too real, too true, too magical,
too endless, too melodious, too holy
a dream, too undefined, too life-giving;
you cannot be an imagery.
Imageries are dull realities,
these are unfaithful, unmoored and
dusty.
I have no place for you there.
I don't cherish to be restless without you.
I don't cherish to be enwrapped in ghastly,
loathsome imageries
or
dull realities.

Confessions Of A Modern Anchorite

Non-facts I dress up as facts,
and feel victory is mine,
my conflicts with comprehension,
absorption, glaring,
and you like me no end.
My love for you has ended long ago when
I fictionalized facts pushing them
out of circulation,
and I caviled at the thoughts of being there,
as the ultimate in the twists and turns of
my confessions.
My greatest moments, hidden beneath
subliminal acts
of deception,
while I jettison my reaches
leaning on the lights of my eyes.

When you go to sleep,
I would move into you
to fetch from you the
price of the confessions
I have just made.

You would soon see my confessions
fading away,
my shapes eloping,
the dismissiveness of stories
lithoidal, about me
and also extinguishing figures
I create in my confessions.

All through I have allowed doses of selfishness
and vanity overpower my puniness,
and when I talk eloquently,
I prosper on the fragility of your madness.

She Amid The Rains At Midnight

1

The sky, inkier,
clouds mesmerizing the
events inside them.
The "Fair-silvered-buskined Nymphs"[1]
above, there,
quietly seized me with their
oddities, disgorging.
I felt uniquely inspired to
be one with those nymphs
I, once, was intimidated with.
The worn-out sensations visited me
in interruptions, fussily,
to gauge the depths of clouds.
The broody plans kept hovering
around the empty corners.
I kept tiptoeing the brightened rays of hope.

2

Peeved at the
early demise of their own colours,
sanguine rainbows commenced
their wanderings towards colourless sky.
The sun now, so elusive, appears
and disappears, kaleidoscopically,
as if the circle would never stop.
Frosty air sabotaging ceaselessly
the pious efforts to breathe insanity
of breathlessness, perverse,

---

[1] Milton in *Arcades*.

omnipresent.
To me the slow pitched sounds of
falling rains resembled the
memories, live and crawling,
of sounds of mysterious footsteps
she came with
in the murkier hours of my
debris.
She laughed twice, once she
was formed and again once
I was deformed but on both
the downpours lavishly
reminded me of the verisimilitudes
of my illusions,
painfully peaked.

3

The drops wiped out successfully
the wetted eyes alluring
something I could never know.
Melancholic, dingy drops
kidded around, gleefully,
waiting for the morning to settle
down.
I saw her shadows
overshadowed by the figure emanating
from the thick clouds.
Ferocious winds howled and howled
threatening the
drops hanging in the air,
fearing earth would soak these up.
Cicadas silenced the smoky hug
I thought of receiving from the
departing wishes, I silhouetted,
remembering their immutabilities.
But the wishes before they eloped

with the rains promised yet another
rendezvous with me, at another midnight
when rains bless her and curse me.

Etiolated Desires

All through I noticed my insides being
rolled out,
a bleak desire overshadows me
and I tell my tears to
smile at their fate.

Curvous desires do shrink, again and
again, but my mirrors don't reflect these.
Awesomeness of unmet happiness,
impeccable, falls flat,
waking me up shamelessly.

Let me now, at least, shed my
despondency, for a while.
Moments, never discerned moments,
wait avidly for their turn in life
to unfold.

A melancholic hush descends
sumptuously, egging me on
to be one with the desires
I live by,
etiolated desires to live by.

Life And Rhythms

The rhythmic occurrences wantonly
meet, in complete isolation,
prophesying the jerky arrival of hissing
realities.

Yearning for charmed disbeliefs swarms
around, in utter disgrace, unnerving the
significant desires, trapped in knotty
perspectives.

The rainbows, so glaring in the night,
fabricate the wily avatars they assume,
when the dusk is on the prowl, slyly,
hoping to reach the deniable silhouettes.

Streaming down,
the rhythms assail the enraptured words
surrendering themselves before
an insignificant, innocuous audience.

Audiences, benumbed minds,
their exquisite desires,
achieve the incomprehensibilities of the
befuddling voices, not so rhythmic.

Archives of unvisited consequences
engrave the tender disenchantments
flowing relentlessly from the replica
of shadowy glimpses, dark and blurred.

Virtuous dichotomies wobble round
the worries across the whole

mind, ragged mind, devoid of all the
sensitivities of the tired heart.

Inert immoralities, their scary
eyes, half-open and half-closed,
restlessly continuing in foggy
darkness to search untruthful rhythms.

Masking the tense symbols of hard
emotions beneath the creamy veneer
mythic tales abound in, the rhythms,
nevertheless, go astray, for a while.

Selfless conjunctions torpedo the rhythms,
spreading their roots, deep-roots
into the sagacious
incapacitations of we human beings.

Fathomable horizons, at times, besmirch
the hallowed designs where we feel assured
of the failures of unseen rhythms,
completing the life cycle.

Tamed Life In Clouds

There, in the dullness of flying clouds or near these,
I was searching the shades of desperations,
floating,
between the top of heaven and
bottom of earth,
upon which sailed
the savory desires of the life, lived and unsavory desires
of the life, unlived.

The clouds stooped suddenly, breaking into
fragmentary segments of fatalistic fixities.
I stood firm, enkindled.
Sublimity of the unbewailing illuminations ensuing
the fading mists of false,
unknown virtues welcomed me.

Appearing and disappearing,
disappearing and appearing,
the clouds, coyly guarded the guiltless indulgences,
I cherished madly and unfaithfully,
through the unlived life destiny desired me
to live afterwards.

Trembling and scrambling,
not trembling and unscrambling,
the clouds through their very earthly eyes gazed at the
tameness of the life,
that very tameness,
blessing the nocturnal brightness
constituted around the life, I never lived.

Beginning and continuing,
ending and not continuing,

the clouds sought unperceived, coiled up hopes,
amid the abundance of aged, myopic turmoil the
life revolved around.

Dispersing asunder,
dissolving into measureless shapes,
emerging from the gaps,
carrying burden of listless life,
the clouds went crazy about the nodding
truths of life,
laurelling magnificently.

An Unfinished Journey

1

We write our most beautiful lines
in solitude of two extremes,
one that reveals nothing, posing no
threat to us and
the other that secretes compulsive
self-revelations.
We are detached from none of the two
but utility of detachment is one thing
and futility of detachment another,
both extending to each other,
both quarreling with their own form,
both vying with each other
both obsessed by pushy self-questionings
of their very own.
We live in these two extremes,
separately, lacking in,
"a dialogic relationship".[1]

2

Like you, I also know that there are times
to feel a sort of sadness
that comes not alone but with a burning
solitude prisoning all of us together,

---

1 Mikhail Mikhailovich Bakhtin, Russian thinker propounded what is referred to as "dialogic relationship" with a view to explain the relationship between two realms which human beings treat as separate. It is this dialogic relationship or double-voiced relationship that is intrinsic to the understanding of inner interpretation in an unified subject.

enabling us think and feel alike, sometimes,
bringing to the fore uniqueness of all
together.
My friends,
we never grip those moments, the gaping
moments we never break open and come out.
Perhaps, we look for reasons of our sadness
and collapse together,
not realizing that a single collapse implies
heartless civilizations become more and more
uncivilized.
But history moves on,
as usual.

3

Whenever I endeavourer to speak about
ruins of our "analogous mass phenomena"[2]
the multitudes of today we put on us
silence me,
torpedoing my carefully selected words
that have descended upon me from the graves
of forgotten, long, languid memories,
coming to me alive,
in different variants,
some seen, some unseen,
some felt, some unfelt,
leaving me devastated,
tempting me to think
as to of what use these memories would be
for those who would be resting in the graveyards
of jumbled tomorrows.

---

[2] Carl Gustav Jung in his essay, the fight with the shadow, talks of this phenomenon to indicate that psychic phenomena are not only confined to individuals alone but also affect a number of different individuals simultaneously with the result that disturbance of the collective phenomenon can be traced in every individual.

4

Against times that never go our way
we weep after the events
hoping for the resurgence of times
that are withdrawn,
and we refusing to go back to
primeval instincts
universally flowing.
Can we escape from our own body,
so venerated?

5

Once I thought, foolishly, meekly,
wherefrom light comes out of covered clouds
when earth is sleeping,
sun is weeping,
madness is at its peak.
The kingdom is shaken,
the stars of yesteryears are pearled in
years yet to ensue.
Let us rid ourselves of
the figures curved in our unconscious
for, what stay there
would consume my ink for my poems.
My poems would peer through
our unconscious
to unlearn the mysteriously written lessons.

6

Dream-walking figures move
pusillanimously,
into the inroads made for them.
Capricious obscurities block them
from within,
they feel tempted, driven, enfeebled,

still walk down the jerky paths
clasped shut with their misty self.
Their weight has suddenly exceeded
and some times, we feel tempted, driven,
dwarfed, walking over their exceeded weight.
Neither they nor we shape our
image,
the image poised so ambivalently,
and we think of others as fools.

7

Once again,
our savageries elude themselves
even through the mirrors,
we hang before ourselves.
Having charred us to live death,
so immaculately shameless choices
echo the arrival of yet another generation
carrying virulently blazing dreams
on their unimaginative visages.
That undying hand surfaces again,
again and again,
giggling at the absent unanimity
of rancid fabrics that make us
survive, for our sake,
yours and mine matter not.
What flies in and out of everyone of us
remains a sad mystery
that armless hand plays with.

8

Look at those wrong deprivations bemoaning
their existence,
the crucified deprivations,
tell us,

meaninglessness does not imply uselessness,
none soils the other,
but none goes together,
ensuring imminent, monotonous calmness
that we gloss over, as is our wont,
for our sake, the sake of our
inner inferno.
Enduring happiness.

9

Our dwellings are disintegrated,
we are the voyagers seeking ourselves
in a world, ruled by inviolate sighs,
delusional ones, destroying.
In dream-like surroundings, the lines
I wish to pen are the lines I sacrifice
for our sake,
thinking, perhaps rightly, the gods of
today sojourn in taverns of tomorrow.
In the dwellings of ours
meet us those traces of enraptured
fractures which define, for us, at last,
what we have cherished to know, for that long,
I mean, why bigger hypocrites rule lesser
ones.

10

We are fictitious people.
We are feeble people,
we live by ourselves alone.
We are crippled people,
we live by our holes.
We are inverted people,
we live by our live ghosts.
We survive by impressions alone;

oblivious of what is distinguishable is separable.[3]
Insoluble riddles.

11

Our single lives have many eras,
each era interspersed with others,
reminding us of ruthless elements
binding the eras mightily,
letting the combined demonic
wisdom, we have inherited,
inspire us to go in for inexorable
defilements.
Sometimes, we are told, these very elements
foam hellishly,
snatching from us our simplicity
luring us to be debased by our own
tempests of self-reflections,
we wallow in so soberly.
We are too inimical to ourselves,
time has taught us so.

12

There, in vacant spaces, old banyan
trees talk and reason,
about our mental prison,
our psychological treason,
our pathological vision.
They ask heavens
to look down upon us, all of us,
as most of us play all games, throughout,
to reach there, ultimately,

---

[3] David Hume's well-known dogma, what is distinguishable is separable; all impressions, being distinct and separate have no logical connections among themselves and therefore these are not unified whole.

to seek final solace
from ourselves, from all our activities.
The banyan trees have resolved now,
they wouldn't entreat heavens any longer,
for heavens too weep
over the absurdities of their fate.

13

While the reminiscences of days of yore
and the distinctions that set them apart,
lead us to the fossilized land of mystique,
we keep asking others wonderingly;
have we not lost our infertilities, our
infantile infertilities to joyful trivialities
of our faith,
our fragmentary suppression,
our swayed concealments,
our inoffensive disconnections,
our separated existence,
our existential partings,
our unforgettable sagas,
our strangulating paths,
our duplicitous exercise of powers,
and perhaps of our changed times?

14

None clarifies some questions,
some questions defy clarifications,
for they create confusion and
on that confusion, restless confusion,
rests the world.
We rest on the world.
We are detached creatures,
born of the womb of restless questions,
we chatter around such questions
and fanatically slip into the deluge

of cowering submission,
to those who have done nothing
but to drift toward the ivory tower
they lodge in.

15

Oh my God, what have you done to our
forgetfulness,
it is on the verge of breaking
and absorbing those malodorous moments
that once held us together.
Now we abhor bracing each other,
we reaffirm our faith in our
being known as the children of
dead era.
We are viciously caught between
the unexplored memories, collective,
and our individual amorphousness.
Possessed as we are of our pangs,
we keep softening ourselves,
hoping one day the vicious circle
would end, ending our self-pity.

16

You people believe in unfathomable
powers of abyss of depthless minds
writing their purest thoughts on
miseries, pains, sadness and turmoil,
horded carefully in besieged corners.
And you people call it
poetry, prose, essay, criticism.
Have you ever seen a vacant face,
peaky, carrying loathsome inertia of
neglect and suffocation,
seclusion and dejection,

in those words, sometimes joyous,
sometimes sober?

17

Unsullied by the fierceness of stillness
which forces itself on all of us, from time to time,
making us stand in grotesquely attired
life we carry with us since time unknown,
we long to live another life, knowing not where
it lies,
what it is and
how it ought to be lived.
Endless impurities hold us disjointedly,
as we walk along unplanted life,
thinking one day we will reach there and
then gossip about what we came for
and what we are going for.
But in vain.

18

What is that which wakes us amid
legless darkness?
What is that which flocks around us
on our moving toward ourselves?
In that paling light what elopes with our
shadows?
We fight with our structures, cheatingly,
our dim interiors in collusion with
our bright exteriors
getting along well,
to reach the point of complete meaninglessness
where exist only we, our and us
and also coexist the formless frame
we would be fitting into
soon.

19

Overawed, we are in constant search of
deadening shadows
that push us farther and farther toward
the floating relationships
we keep breaking, on small pretexts.
We forget, that even after our death
what separates us out are the shadows
that kept haunting us, when alive.
That sound of restless years, that have
elapsed, keeps many doors ajar for us,
we never enter these
for we are afraid of brooding over
drooping sounds
that come from our nebulous memory.

20

Our lives like our deaths live in exile.
Our remembrances live in exile
as do our amnesias,
and we believe we have lived
full life and died fully.
Mistaken notions overcome us
and we are completely ebbed
pretending to grope
between unoozing light and oozing
darkness.
Broodingly.

21

Dure ways are always open
to those who pronounce judgments
without knowing what they are,
trying to catch up with frozen
disenchantments.

We sleep, as usual,
letting trembling dawn fade into
exhausting morning.
We stay unprofaned,
trying to overpower
the isolations that lie disembogued
in night's possessiveness.
Our deep-throated laughter
more often than not
sucks the water inside our skull
and make us more agile.

22

My sufferings have ceased to be meaningful
at least for me, for the time being,
for I have failed to make out a cause out of
these.
My sufferings do reconnoiter the outer
surfaces my foolish memories have.
My memories are not desensitized till now
but are indeed sick, it seems,
sickness would soon melt into
death.
"In the slave market of my melancholy mind
I mount the auction block
To sell myself to the highest bidder of misery."[4]
You would soon discover purposeful
sufferings are no less grieving than
purposeful glee,
both are sacrificed for his mercy,
one pains and the other
pains too.

[4] Lines from Joseph Cowen's poem.

23

Something floats up, miserly, and then
dwindles suddenly.
From within you are facile,
like a tiny ray of light,
groping reluctantly within that
gigantic mass of hovering darkness.
We, in our wisdom, slither around you
and come nowhere near ourselves.
The domes of your sanity digs into
immemorial chapters
of insanity running amok,
of discretion sitting on barrage,
of secret rooms staying privy to exclusiveness,
of seclusions glowing among harsh
mental leeches.
We lament the dilapidated kingdoms of dead kings
and unusable bedrooms of languid queens.

24

Stunningly disgusting are the ways
men resolve their absurdities
inhabiting pulverized lands spreading
beyond our dreams.
We go sick.
And then roll through bizarreness of
wobbling innocence
that came our way in our childhood.
Emptiness of our youth descends on
us coolly leading us to the outer edges
of madness.
Our paranoia is complete now.
We have suddenly become sane entities,
enjoying our drinks, our food, our culture
and our deranged sojourners too.

25

In looking forward to meeting
life fulfilling prophesies,
we tread the lands that once impoverished
us, as ruthlessly as we did
when brute darkness refused to
show us the way.
My shadowy acquaintances, hear me,
we never go in for searching roads
lying so naked inside our awaken infancy
we, rather, heedlessly pursue the displaced
agony.
I am afraid,
symbols and allusions have colluded
with our betrayals,
we are no longer what our forefathers
intended us to be.

26

Alimented upheavals, myriad illuminations
resolve the mythical mysteries,
alternating between the lost and the losable,
fainting innocence of unsung dirge and sung
miseries,
call you repeatedly, loudly, bemusing,
you flutter your eyelids
looking at the eloquence of the dry earth.
You wouldn't ridicule the scarce demands
of the unsaid, unuttered
desires.
Mean obscenities, centuries later,
come hopping but come too late.
Useless blank visages tell us an altogether
different story where
exist none, neither you nor I, neither he nor she,
but only our drifting horizons.

27

All along the pimpled lives we have lived
we, all of us, I mean, stop somewhere
to introspect, for a while, about the endless
darkening stupidities we possess,
wavering between streams of coordinated
successes and uncoordinated failures,
talking stagnantly of our blind perusal
of veneered paths,
we have betrayed ourselves with,
shutting ourselves up in the impoverishing
yearning for trivial-looking fame,
that smiles at some of us,
with others weeping over their lost desires.
Some desires have darker birth,
others not.

28

Some of us, on verge of nervous wreck,
some as hale and hearty as a newly deceased
body,
we lead together the juggernaut
that aspires for a better place, a safer place,
a conscientious place,
where circles may not have many and many
sub-circles, each sub-circle set in a secret
connivance against others.
Strange, though it might seem,
it defies all logics, stony and bald alike,
that make us intelligent and prudent
but inward looking,
that living in sub-cycles makes us no more
rational than the broken bundle
of unknown curios.

29

Coherence of incoherence or
incoherence of coherence
tiptoe each other, hoping, better
sense would dawn on us someday
unsettling our enigmatic forays into
ourselves,
making us realize,
things lying outside us are more
enchanting, exhuming, exhausting
than the ones that have ruled us,
for too long,
from within.
The days ahead are the days
bringing, together the nights
that have gone, staying awake,
contemplating over the times
when stars used to smile
over the rush of light over darkness.

30

When in deep sleep, he comes to me,
not always, occasionally,
with his wrinkled obsessions and my
ochre desires and tells me his stories
of merciful relations he once enjoyed
with me, with all of us, separately,
and before he departs he cautions me
of what would soon claw at those
relationships,
which once were in deep flames,
clamouring for layers of haunted lights
unable to open up.

31

"Where are you, my prodigious stars?"
What a wonderful age we are in, with
wonderful men and women unsettling
their trusts toward each other.
We walk toward each other, unwelcome,
unwanted and at times unperturbed.
We have still not stopped hating others
who matter not for us
and for those who really matter
we simply don't exist.
We have measured our existence
in terms of declining values.
Dazzling indeed.

32

Wry smiles, the mystics display,
in order to become acceptable
to those who believe in austere glimpses
our gods display, resting our hopes on
possible self-actualization of illusions,
millions and millions years old bleak,
innocent, illusions,
self-imposed,
super-imposed,
causing us no uneasiness,
trapping us in our dissembled identities,
completely buoyed up.
Those tiny, opalescent parts don't get
fused together.
The juggernaut moves on.

33

Musing upon the rocky monoliths
they watch the world and its various
colours.

They see Ganga, the revered river, being
worshipped by dry men and dry women,
dirty dogs and their leprous masters
washing off their sins,
hoping to get along well in next life.
Their sins would flow as flows Ganga,
somewhere in subterranean waters
she is living, alone, with her miseries
intact and loneliness all pervading.
She has been logical, to herself, to all of us,
she has refused to surface,
for good.

34

Those waiting anonymously for countless
centuries,
land there, again and again,
and tell us their unheard stories of how
they lost their faith in Ganga.
Like us Ganga listens carefully and laments
her lost glory,
when none told her his story,
and all heard her beauteous plunders
spanning centuries and covering vast
concourse of people helplessly grappling
with their grumbling fates.
Well-nigh past are those episodes confirming
our subjugation to our morbidity.

35

Who seeks ultimate expressions of our identity,
with our dubiously attired expressions revealing
homogeneity of every consequence and
heterogeneity of no consequence and
in between lie collective amnesias of priceless
possessions, fuming vigorously?

We confess our failures,
rarely,
we proceed with our psychical impulses,
rarely bothering about melancholies of choice-less
chances
that come and come galore, but for only a few.

36

The lips that sing a song tonight
are the lips
that kissed me years back,
that sipped me years back,
that drank mine years back,
that sabotaged me years back,
that warmed me years back.
But the lips that sing tonight
are not her lips,
these are not the lips which
drew solace for me,
in my moments of solitude,
in my moments of ignominies,
in my moments of torments.
Where are those lips?
Ask, Homer.
I ask Homer.
Homer gives me unowned lips.[5]
I need owned lips.

37

Our greatest strengths glare us in their
totality, weakening our weaknesses
that stand hidden behind our well-crafted

---

[5] Remember the lines from Book XX, Odysseus—Insulted And Protected. "The lips they laughed with seemed as it were not their own...." In Homer's *The Odyssey*.

glasses, black, veiled and too transparent.
We see no glimpses, never, of our villainy
for, our combined youth is still lording over
our concealed death.
We have lost the times to lean over our
lost shadows,
there is no use in weeping over split milk,
inarticulate uprisings within our skulls
keep misting over delinquencies our skulls
never could think of.
Our skulls have paradise of their own
where we at times sit together feeling
the cruel, icy paws of twists and turns of
irremediable errors.

38

Let them think our madness is complete.
Let them also think their sanity is intact.
Let them think we would never meet.
Let them also think our destruction is a fact.
We must see that what deserts us must
come back to us safely,
defying the dictates of the fugitive times
roaring in fragmented voice,
subsiding slowly, reminding us that we have
to set out again toward a disfigured
civilization dancing in delirium,
complete delirium.
Don't dare remembering what cause
these periodic deliriums.
The buried gods are still alive.

39

We never expect clues from what wheel
around us,
those protruding clues bring to us an array

of silently formed connections
from which we question, after a long time,
about why we don't move toward each other.
The maps are peopleless, placeless.
There are only gaping holes there,
we fear entering as if those holes would
confront us with our orotund images
crying hoarse, anguished in colourless
lull.
I don't want to return to you again,
I have ceased to crawl before pygmies,
I would rather die than be killed,
conscientiously.

40

Jarred by the hoariness of movements,
my friends tease me,
asking me why people prefer buffoons to me.
I tell them to read Dante Alighieri.
"Like loves like."
Fallen creatures have webbed a history
of their own,
a history around themselves,
a history which permits no entry
and no exit.
It is a closed history.
Its doors are closed.
Men and women there are not suffocated
but highly suffocating,
they make it sure none other than their ilk
reach the insides of their history.

41

Who does not have a flair for being known?
But to some, unknown-ness comes as a virtue.
In that flair to be known one is never free from

oneness of oneself,
from collusions one is powerlessly tempted to measure
with his expanding ego
that peters out after one is no longer with oneself.
You mean death.
Yes.
We stand aglitter, fighting with our exhaustions,
a lone battle, we know we would lose shortly
but we continue knowing not why.
We have hanged our strangeness somewhere
on our concealed frankness.
We know.
Perhaps.

42

Ambivalence of unrecognized opposites
we have been overlooking,
thinking positively
and toying with the dark visions of light.
It is no longer an exception,
it is, indeed, a fashion.
A haggard fashion.
We are the makers of such fashions,
we extend everywhere.
We wander on continuums,
perhaps to shun our dwindling base
or perhaps to abide by what we never
set for us.
What a massive leaning we have learnt
from our hearkening love for our base?

43

The wholeness of the world is fixated into
my dead eyes,
stemmed to glance at the world that exists
with no beginnings and no ends.

I go on, I go on, searching for the one
who, I believe, will help me retrieve the
light of my dead eyes.
Once I, ever get the light,
I promise I wouldn't run back
to that old, languid world of
sickening creatures,
crying amidst themselves.

44

We also walk through the mesh of ourselves
saving our essence from the havocs of
stiffening retrievals.
That figure, the mesmerizing one, confronts
us, asking us to unbridle the riddles around
our infinite beings.
We say, let us not stroll into our happenings again,
for, our happenings have no distinctions,
no demarcations.
That figure feigns listening.
Lusterless brusqueness falls flat.
We are not ashamed, even now.
We are slowly freezing ourselves.
Ravagers versus ravagers,
that is how we see each other.
And praise each other.

45

Then my fellow travellers, my friends.
Let us not act like members of The Compson Family.[6]

---

[6] William Faulkner's novel *The Sound And The Fury* tackles a family i.e. The Compson family, the members of which lack trust in each other, trying to exploit others; ultimately, completely ruined. The psychological realism in this novel is such that readers find it hard to tell where reality ends and memory begins and the puzzles Faulkner creates for readers continue till the end.

Let us not tread lightly,
we have climbed successfully
the monolithically inclined
pervasiveness.
Let us rewrite, jointly,
those chapters of historical cowardice
standing in queue to get marvelously
tremulous laurels.
Someday, somewhere, we will meet
again and resolve to think sensibly
of how to look back at what we have lost
and of how not to loose these again.
Not a battle of what is lost and what is not,
Not a journey of movement, of continuity,
Not a foray into our functioning,
This long journey, still unfinished,
judges us through our self-questionings.

Random Thoughts

I

Mankind, uncovered in its grandeur,
long laments and their marvelous beauty,
indelible marks on the heart.

II

Philosophers theorize, purposelessly,
treasures of life aflutter,
for the moment no escape from oneself.

III

Deprived of love, logic, reason, vision,
haphazard human relationships,
go side by side in complete confusion.

IV

Our desires fixed in stones, alive,
our nakedness chaotic and complete,
what slumps pathetically is useless.

V

Artistic magnificence and that
mellowing dusk, instant reminder of
voluptuousness, friendly feelings.

VI

Expectations and the passing world,
fully awakened, old anguishes stay
unrelieved, unparallel, unvisited.

VII

A pulverized negation, a lit lamp, a street,
circles, circles, and many more circles,
on wayside lies yet another circle.

VIII

There, in that circle, a formless void
awaits avidly; many more voids
swarm around many circles, dragged.

Eroded Memories

Where are those impulses we survive by?
And also survive by the passions, we keep
to our heart.
Fleeing to some other retreat where odyssey
neither the notions nor the passions,
we cluster around the elf, nameless, faceless.
In deep, intimate moments,
that come once and
that they share with ageless, dulled fallacies,
waiting for the chronicle of devastating muses
to arrive near them;
at their own convenience.

The intensities collude with muffling voices,
raised inside their transcendent ruins,
echoless voices heard, again and again,
voices never hearing their own echo.
Disparaged redeemer,
having guaranteed to
them a place in eternal eventualities,
stare toying with crippled, unveiled quiescence.

Where are those glimpses we survive by?
And also survive by the shuddering visions,
we perch upon.
Don't hide yourself in dwarfed depths.
These are exhausting concealments where odyssey
neither the glimpses nor the visions;
you keep philosophizing
the unusual games of innocence and ignorance,
concealments exhausted.

Those cruel, restless hands come to us; our
passions, our glimpses and our visions
suddenly elope in the abyss of darkening,
festering memories;
eroded since time immemorial.

These can never be dethroned, never enthroned,
their insufferable notions and infallible glimpses
defend disjointed contrasts,
construed notions,
obtruded glimpses,
held ransom in eroded memories.

Seeking Solace In An Empty Room

I stood in an empty room
but couldn't find sun rising,
air flowing, rains falling,
winds blowing, sands flying,
leaves drying, birds singing,
moon sinking, stars falling,
children weeping, girls singing.
I still wait.
So does the room, though it
has become more empty,
more matured for, it has learnt
that its wait would never end.
And it solaces it.
It calms it.
I stood in an empty room
waiting for the frozen emotions
to defrost,
for silent music to wander like
unbridled streams,
for trembling edges to firm up
their exactitude,
for tranquilized sadness to melt
slowly.
I still hope to wait.
So does the room.
Empty, though it is.
It has an unshakable faith in
its own emptiness, in its own
invincibility, in its own recesses.
The attractiveness of hollowness that

lives with me throughout there,
enchants me, befuddles me, coaxes me,
telling me interruptedly
that there are many other rooms more
empty than this room.
Why?
Can it be so?
Yes.
Because the ones in those rooms are
more emptied than the rooms.

Artless Art

Art without creativity is futile,
art with creativity is fragile,
both meddling with each other,
without continuum, continuing,
with memory flowing like time
catching up with itself.
Darkness zeroing in on light,
light zeroing in on darkness,
fusion zeroing in on confusion,
confusion zeroing in on fusion.
Background submerging into figure,
figure submerging into background.
Pyrrhus's ring and its stone;
needed no art.[1]
Everyone knows.
Soulless countours worthlessly
dismember in a directionless
direction,
longing for immutable equilibriums,
while artless art implodes,
untriumphantly,
within itself.

---

[1] Pliny says that in Pyrrhus's ring there was a stone that had the figure of Apollo and the nine Muses in the veins of it. He further tells that there was no help from art in its production.

Riot And The Young Lady

Roads, long and narrow, blood-bathed roads
and their stifling skins yield chaos, dusty,
shaming the strayed sunshine and creating an
inspiring misgivings about others.
They treasure the mess, the happenings give
birth to, asking for more and more such mess,
and longing to intrigue against the slackened
inclinations of love and affiliation.
Irrelevancies cry about the relevancies,
that have decided to move in suffocating silence
promising to return back as memories come back
to normalcy after the burial of the dead.
Dimmed eye's refusal to retrieve lost tears
grew stern, lighting, half-heartedly, the hopes
lying so low underneath the corpses, forgotten for
long, as they have no takers.
The passions that ruled last week are dead now,
the emotions that splashed last week are dismayed now,
the blood that boiled till recently is icy cool now.
Floating, floating and floating are our senseless
voices, languid and wearisomely agile voices.

The young lady looking outrageously old,
fragile and thoughtful,
walks slowly,
stops,
searches,
moves.

Disheveled,
amnesic,
dammed,

folding unmindfully,
scudding against herself,
the young lady swiftly clusters herself.

Who is this lady?
Sybil[1] hell bent on writing a new chapter of history.
"Who would remember the history you people
wrote last week? Would you or you or you or who else?"
mutters that lady,
her inhibitions, standing shy, nearby.

Nightmares soften their stand now,
they don't choke now,
for they adore the light of the day now.
Their very symbols savagely mourn
the brutish supremacy of strangulating encroachments
over what couldn't be revived now,
never.

Reddish traces linger on
and that young fragile looking lady,
lost in her remembrance,
like an unnoticeable cog
in the gargantuan past called
precious history,
and suddenly asks:
"That's vile—should we a parent's faults adore,
And err, because our fathers err'd before?"[2]

Their tones become menacing,
wrong reasons wiping out right ones,
antiquated philosophers usurp their
forgotten inertia as if
the young lady would soon lose her fragility.

---

[1] Women, who in ancient times, used to predict events. A witch also.

[2] Charles Churchill in *The Rosciad.*

Dreams Versus Realities

We live within our dreams,
our redeeming facts of life,
outside, in a state of chaotic indifference;
realities have emerged
victorious, putting fantasy into action.

The straying of our dreams,
the straying of our realities,
disdainfully immeasurable,
severity of either seems appallingly short,
fulfilling and slippery.

Dreams pattering out of...?
smile jejunely,
being our worst enemies,
they leave us when we need realities the most.

The realities enthrall us,
The dreams disenthrall us,
The dreams logic with realities,
The realities never.

Dreams go to the bottom of inverted irrationalities;
our grandeur glares at our blighted enormity
skillfully constructing around us the heights of utopia,
we have lived thus far, pathetically.

The garb the realities fear,
The dreams never wear.
The realities have their lot,
The dreams not.

We are living people, for,
we are obscured lot, quarrelling with our
obscurity,
we are wondrous lot, rejoicing our
malignancy,
we are discordant lot, wandering here and there,
looking through our morbidity into
what come in our dreams,
we are disillusioned lot, seeking illusions
into legion meanings of dreams,
measuring the distance from realities.

Oneness is not ownness.
Ownness is not oneness.
What wanes faster, unknown.
Barren innocence,
taken for a ride.

Dreams don't hold our hands,
our hands are free and unrestrained,
realities do hold our hands,
we fear our hands.

Dreams and realities prowl,
ruminate, reinforcing
sadness of life and awaking us
to realities, we live by.

Far and deep down,
realities flow forwards,
dreams flow backwards,
clumps of haze welcome both,
on their bidding adieu to each other.

For My Friends And Foes Alike

I know I made a promise to myself,
I would do justice to that promise,
I would unfurl what I have seen and
listened, perceived and received.
Today that time has come, the time
to unfold the uncombed assimilations.
I have trapped so many things within me,
Yes, my friends and my foes alike,
my day of reckoning has come,
I will open a new world before you,
a world you chaps have lived for long,
without having been mirrored,
without being aware of your own reflections.
Don't seek your salvation, divinity,
your joyful existence pales into insignificance,
insignificance unleashed by your individuality.
So, my dear friends and my dearer foes,
again alike,
don't feel offended, exhumed, exhausted,
kill me, abhor me, abuse me, declare me a moron,
but, for the sake of yourself, read this poem.

My friend and my foes,
you are in a complex whirlpool
of the events and of persons and of talks
and of drinks and of foods and of circumstances
and of heroic deeds and of value premises and
of epidemics of conflicts and of doubts and of
illusions and of disillusions and of unchallenged
hopes and of everything that happens there,
freely and amazedly,
that place we call a place for our survival.

Don't get gripped by panic,
you wouldn't, I know for certain,
your skin has thick layers of self-deception,
your vanity propels you, it drives, it directs.
You are, indeed, a purposeless creature,
rejoicing in the purposelessness of your being.
Triumphantly.

Under your calmposed reverie
lie plethoric abnormalities,
and stoutly protected delusions.
And also instinctive intuitions
tyrannized by your fears.
You need not flounder,
unnecessarily,
your stilted intelligence has already
oozed out of the casks your self-deception
has created for you, for your rest.
I dare not exhort you,
for, you don't consider me worthy
of your solemnized disgust.
But, this time, my solemnized soul and I
would extract the best of the worst
of you.
At my own peril, indeed.

My loathing, my satires, my strains
come and block my path,
they tell me about the way you have
been undone
or you have undone yourself.
This is a big question, lurking as lurk
you in your delirium.
I am not prudent; I know it,
but my prudence is not without sheen,
imprudence is strength,
it is all protective, all imperatorial.

I have chilled my imprudence,
now I am at par with you,
totally unified with you, all of you.
I have at last won my creativity.
Still, dears, our dreams don't have the
same meeting grounds,
our dreams don't collapse together.
Yes, that is why I am imprudent.

There are things, destined not to happen,
there are things, desired not to happen,
there are things,
these are things,
which we go to distant past to meet with.
And come without flying colours.
And then we seek solutions in faded stars.
You are locked up man.
Your intellectual sperms are dead.
You can create nothing but deadwood.

Half-truths

Half-truths grieve on the other side of the horizon,
unintelligible acts mould us and raise us to a higher pedestal.
Onlookers say: Gnaw at those oddities that give life to half-truths.
For thousands of years, you rode the blur between what you are and what you are not,
still you believe in immutabilities of imageless half-truths.
These thousands of years have hardened your skin,
your obtrusion into these years would make you more senile,
ambiguity of your inner-being and awfulness of you outer
would wait for you thousands years later.
What has slithered past you?
Just now.
Something arises from that dilapidated debris,
and with trepidation, yells loudly,
"I, the harbinger of your past, will shield you then.
Your isolation is self-imposed; let it peter out."
Pathos rule the roost, for the time being.
Pathos revolve in those harrowing holes in your mind
that you have decided to fill with mirages of intrusive
stories hailing from swirling truths.
The guilty half-truths approach crazily the truths you have dreamed,
and suddenly come across the truths that are aflame,
bizarrely in resonance with what you never allowed to happen
during thousand years that just passed by.
You have a veneer of muteness.
Your answers are multitudinous.
You want us to wait.
You want us to be buried in the ageing vengeance of years,
years, full with stories of truths narrated
in terms of half-truths.

Now you have raised your head again
this time with extracts from the debris
of your antiqued anguish.
And you pose this question,
"When half-truths serve the purpose, why seek truths?"
"Self-appeasement is not my cup of tea, darling."
I retort.
"To hell with you, one day you would be hanging in one
of the gaps, harrowing gaps, that teach us, over the years,
...."
"What?", my patience, extinguished.
You think, for a while, before yowling,
"Don't live by indelible traces.
These traces will make you an enigma unto yourself.
You will be a stranger to yourself.
Aimless, bruised, haphazard...."
Truths share their aches in unison with those of
half-truths,
their mind is furrowed,
all these years, thousands and thousands of years,
have betrayed truths and betrayed half-truths.
What, then, our hopes do hinge on?
On the tenuous relationship
between truths and half-truths.
We look up with longing,
we are perforated,
we look askance at,
and having barred all avenues to half-truths
we have become inscrutably somber.

My School Teacher

He resting on
his pervasive leanness,
his clothes, in their
own warp and woof,
telling me an altogether
different story.

He spoke,
as soberly as coolly,
conveying to me
hypocrisies, woven
executively,
around stories,
books tell,
marvelously.

Whole history of learning
and knowledge,
crafted inside the palaestra
of his forehead,
he bequeathing me hopes:
for off in future
I would be exploring into.

He means to me;
then and now
a continuum of
nuanced thought,
throughout,
since time immemorial,
yet to come to full shape;
unshaped.

In him and him alone,
I got glimpses of
pathetic pages of
callous absurdities
of history
and on such a page,
what came my way was
his existence and mine
nonexistence.

And in between
his existence and
my nonexistence
lay
the rustling
relationship
between
what he gave and
what I found.

Tears Of A Child

A light glow,
night.
A dark gloom,
day.

A child weeps
on a solaceless road,
unheard.

Both the glow
and the gloom
merge.

His tears
represent
merged glow
and merged gloom,
deepening.

Beauty Is Not Enough

That thin lining,
beauty and ugliness,
relations, inseparably
hostile.

A multiple peaked beauty
a single peaked ugliness
logic dies.

Incoherence in beauty
coherence in ugliness,
life jovial,
self-propelling.

In awakened torpor,
beauty is ugliness,
ugliness beauty,
intractably calm.

Our ascended desires,
a hotbed of
beguiling beauty,
at cross purposes
with equally beguiling
ugliness.

Trust

A tree outside the window,
a bird inside its nest,
they lived together
a life, full of inward agility
a trust.

A house beside the tree
a family inside the house,
they lived together
a life, full of outward agility,
a mistrust.

One day,
both the tree and the bird
talked to each other,
perhaps about the
family.

And next day,
there was neither the tree
nor the bird,
their trust,
standing still.

In search of
a new tree,
a new bird.

Thousands years passed;
no tree, no bird.
Inwardness of trust
resting its hopes

on the family and
it's mistrusts.

Hours,
Days,
Months,
Years,
Thousands years.

Hope continues...?

Blissful End

Alas, the youthful exuberance of silence
strikes me too early, too silently.
The detours, I hate and hate, leads me to
a rendezvous with forgotten memories,
shoving themselves upwards.
In the mist of lazy desert,
my unfulfilling days sleep in my
puckered brain, with fantasies, dying and
inspiring.

The curly images, prowl,
these look desperate at the vigour of
their own invincibility, ruthlessness.
Wavering images bamboozle me,
asking me,
"What falls flat to welcome the rising shadows
of the ghosts that rule us?"
Ghosts don't reveal.
Puny chaps don't reveal.

Sometime back, did I not cajole you?
To join me in my odyssey to the land
of blissful encroachments.
And then you complained of my
stirrings riding the panicky
stars, you thought, that jumped from
the sky.

Rocky sentiments revolve round
aimlessly the hedges and the edges
that talk of the centrality of
adventures, misadventures.

Caged tremulous ends rip apart
the dreary thoughts, sometimes pimpled
and sometimes wrinkled.
Unsung plaudits yell tirelessly,
seeing the agony of the end
whose bliss weaves its resignation.

Of Friedrich Nietzsche's "Superfluous People"[1]

My courteous readers; a highly demanding
job has obtruded itself unto myself.
Let me be detached, for a while;
only then, I will explore into fragmentariness,
abrupt fragmentariness of
lives, conflicts, frustrations, failures, hidden oedipal wishes,
emotions, anxieties, impulses,
and above all selfish ends.
Moving and moving towards those ends.
That is life.
And such a life as they lead: a faceless, a featureless
life, a life of adverse reversals,
a life where they forge their anfractuous character,
And Yes, it is such a life that inspires me to penetrate into their
unseizable, jumbled-up life.
I thank them, all of them, thank them for inspirations they give
me to write of people.
Of Friedrich Nietzsche's "Superfluous People".
All of us have met;
have we not?

My esteemed readers,
I, like all of you, have lived, one time or the other,
with and among stones, both men and women.
I, like all of you, have walked along, one time or the other,
with and among stones, both men and women.
Intelligent men, de-etherized,

---

[1] Nietzsche's develops the concept of 'Superfluous People' in *Thus Spoke Zarathustra*.

Beautiful women, odoriferous.
Stones we move with,
We move with stones.
Like a frog remembering his days while
in hibernation,
I, too, remember those days, those moments,
the days, the moments, the people,
the superfluous people.
We move among stony creatures.
Creatures with their anonymously
myopic depths.

What an obscured welcome those moments
bring to me,
through hitch-hiked associations,
bringing me activities,
delightful activities, garbed insensibly
and masked sensuously.
Really delightful.
A long, languid, loathsome, lulling
chill,
awaiting the incomers, all going into
that big whirlpool, the big hall.

A crow caws;
Suddenly many crows caw.
An owl, dancing owl, yells, usual voice,
"I rule the roost."
Juggernauts may join the chorus.
That loner cautions HIM.
"So what." retorts HE.

The soliloquist propels further towards himself,
and meets,
the lethal conspiracy of
their thoughts, deeply ensconced in
a blind alley.

A camera obscura.
And soliloquizes,

"Why should I evaluate, reevaluate
things around me?
Is it my business?
We wouldn't alter; change is not
our forte. We, human beings, would
not change; our past, present, future
are unalterable and we, an immutable
part of our past, our present and our
future, solicit separation from this artistic
stillness; we wouldn't change."

Jagged frailty surges between
grandeur movements and decapitated
whispers,
horrid passions
and beseeching gestures.
There are men imbued with
intelligence
and there are women soaked with melting
beauty,
both creating a world after their own images.

That buxom woman,
her architectural contours,
lips, oversized, enveloping,
eyes, devilishly inviting,
a treat for connoisseurs, then,
a boring spinster, now,
wriggling her huge hips,
giggles,
with an air of abstraction.

The rapturing magic and music,
the ecstatic sex and crime,

slipping into dismembering
cauldron of false retreat,
as he muses his deceitful, deceptive
muse.

That short, bearded, ebrious, anglicized adult
still a bachelor, beats the drum as if
a chimpanzee beats its chest, in anger,
and suddenly raises his short hands upwards
as lewd music flows.

The fantasizer, standing nearby,
keeps fantasizing.

Wrong, wrong, wrong.
Stones don't melt.
We are all wrong,
with our mutilated musings.
I saw hoarded words hanging between
their laughter and their noisy quietude,
between the continuities
of retiring relevancies and discontinuities of
trickling irrelevancies.
Quenched imageries,
elegantly borne smiles,
fizzily enjoyed pleasures,
stymieing ruminations,
flourishing versifications.
What a delightful place it is?

The woman, Ms G, her gorgeous legs,
and her broken marriage.
Reason?
Ms G reasons, face uncomfortably serious,

"Marriage, a disordered arrangement,
a cocoon, a sheltered existence.
You seek order in it.

You succeed, you have children;
You fail, you have divorces.
You neither succeed nor fail,
You have both"

Two spectacled men, adult ones,
and their grand entry.
One tells,
"I am more intelligent."
Shouts the other,
"No, No, I am more."
And then they burst into
boisterous laughter, together, a sheepish laughter.
But what the argument is for?
Who is more intelligent?

Their minds and their harsh howling,
disembogued howling.
Stones do melt.
Reaping their laurels.
So are these intelligent men.

After all, there are men enjoying the
craftiness of their lengthened miasma
and there are women rejoicing at their
dappling beauty.
Flairs of flamboyance
so impotently on display.
Shaking his head meditatively and looking at
the bosomy girl, he smiled, nonchalantly.

The loner keeps soliloquizing,
remembering his not too distant a past,

"In these parties I was unwelcome as I have always been, so unusual it was,
when she came rushing to me, reminding me of those few months
I spent with Mr N and his wife, made for each other, rarely

staying together, that made them a happy and prosperous couple;
and then requesting me why should I not open my mouth;
now at least let words fall from my silence portraying the gentleman
who had damaged, as she told me magnanimously, the
entire fabric
of gentlemanliness, sophistry, honesty, ethics, equity, the
moral assets
the poker-faced chap left no opportunities to brag about as
his jeweled possessions.
My knowledge must not conflict with my shyness as more
often than
not failure of this leads to the success of the likes of Mr N and if
I did not open my dry lips that night, what a great injustice
would ensue
would be beyond imagination and inert ruffians like him would
keep prospering throughout in times to come and though I was a
ruined man, by all accounts and no big deals would, in any case,
come my way, I must neither fear nor dither in exposing
that man,
for good.

I felt enthused, my dear readers, to confess it to you; to lay
before you,
all of you, how I met this man and also a few of his ilk,
men I would describe as extraordinarily wily and calculating,
who had learnt all vital lessons of upward mobility, of
course, amid
ignominies of the worst sort.
It would, indeed, be in the fitness of the things that I first introduce
you, my revered readers, to that man whose might was to
occupy the
childish imagination of many sycophants, at least for a few limited
years the last of which would see that wretched inane nob
in possession
of an important position. I would then set about to narrate
how they killed

the genuine labours they felt threatened with, in order to be in safety.

They behaved jointly as do behave a pack of jungle dogs,
in thinking alike before they decide the tricks of the game
to reach their targets thinking not even a bit of what others
and there are umpteen number of people with decency left
in their intellect, would think of these tricks.

The poker-faced lowbrow, Mr N, I have mentioned earlier, to me, appeared
like an enigmatic animal fox, gestures revealing no true intentions,
Fond of parties, late night ones, an ogler of the first water,
when every one present had entire
times of the world, free times, with them that they intended to divert
for the purposes they acquired the most during the useless years
of their lives lived thus far.
They had learnt throughout...."

Oh Shit! (Sorry...thought process disconnected.)

But who moves there, in that corner?
An indistinct figure, talking, as always,
on her mobile.
sudden laughter, very loud,
definitely not a gender sensitive lady.
Pl...e...a...s...eeee, S...i...rr,
She screeches,
her yellowish, protruding teeth loosely fixated
in pinkish gum, in full display.
She talks, talks and talks; mobile and its
mobility.
"Haaaaa...aaaaaa...aaa."
or
"Hon...Hon...Hon...aaaaa."

trying to attract young youth; pats him,
alas! too late, she being 47, now.

The words get hummed into my ears,

"I sought to share
the life of snow
and fire.
But neither snow nor fire
took me in."[2]

and I tell this semi-old lady; you missed your marriage,
and you missed the life of snow and fire,
keep talking on telephone; you are half lunatic,
very soon you would be full,
you, a big liability, must not become bigger one,
keep talking.

Such men and such women.
Their brains, etherized,
much before they are born.
Stones possess similar traits.
Vagueness reigning supreme
on their wild, rigid visage.
Men drowning
themselves in never-finishing pegs of
romanticizing water of life,
and women, bulging and hugging
their vapory realities;
hallucinating them totally.

That bulky, sad, gloomy, google-eyed man,
sips his first one, a drunkard,
his restlessness in complete evidence,
a falsified notion overtakes him,

---

[2] Ali Ahmad Said alias Adonis, a Syrian poet in his poem 'The Passage'. (Translated by Samuel Hazo)

he, known for having managed his wife
the way mammoth disasters are managed,
sips another and then talks loudly of
"gender issues in disaster management".

Ms S impressing the gathering
with her outpourings, loud enough to be heard,
"Husbands are abstract
faces in frames. Hang them anywhere
and that is their place."
Mr S ogling at his colleague's young daughter;
he has had an affair with young daughter's
mum, long back.

His mind, obsessed with,
"her pure and eloquent blood
Spoke in her cheeks, and so distinctly wrought,
That one might almost say, her body thought."[3]
and that young daughter refreshing Mr S' memories.
"Like mother, like daughter."
murmurs Mr S, despondently.

Soliloquizing continues; that loner, a detached chap,
a totally unwelcome guest,

"In my last meeting, I told that young lady,
You talk of relations, relations, you
have just talked of.
I know relations as I never got one.
Relations stay well,
undefined,
uncovered by boundaries,
limitations not binding these,
not containing meanings.

---

[3] John Donne in *The Second Anniversary.*

Relations that have boundaries, that have meanings
are beautifully threatened relations; these overawe."

And he continues, as Ms G and Ms S sip their gin,

"Most lovely relations exist between two
human beings; two human beings are no
fathers, no mothers, no brothers, no sisters,
no lovers, no beloveds, no sons, no daughters…
just two human beings…, two persons,
no defined relations..."
and that young lady, as always, kept wavering her head,
nodding in agreement, perhaps.

Oh! My Gosh,
the three women represent the whole,
one six feet tall; an other six feet tall;
and this tiny rogue, an established alcoholic,
four feet eight inches,
the show held abroad.
That tiny rogue' tiny hubby,
an eunuch, a sperm-less creature,
looking for solace,
in pornography, not finding it there,
laughs loudly like a bastard.
That loner cautions HIM.
They will misrepresent YOU, Sir.
"So what." retorts HE.

Tyrannical supremacy
of ideas,
carnal and fallacious,
reigning supreme.
Culmination of spiritless desires
and their imprudence,
benign looking faces, some grave
and some not so grave

coming together,
disjointedness, the process completed.

That short, bearded, ebrious, anglicized adult,
still a bachelor, beats the drum as if
a chimpanzee beats its chest, in anger,
and suddenly raises his short hands upwards
as lewd music flows.

They converse haughtily,
they laugh flightily,
they express concerns,
they voice unuttered words.

Stones don't experience the essence of things,
in this place, a marvelous place, at that.
Their imagination and its
unmistakable agony.
That lofty grace and that unwrapped beauty,
flowering into conceit, tempting them to agree
with what they never agreed on.
Passionate about their own conveniences,
scandals, pluralities and vexing attitudes
their pampering atrocities stand outraged.
Extraordinary persons with ordinary dreams.
Ordinary persons with extraordinary realities.
Ambitions vying variously, to get a glimpse
of the sagging master;
lost in the debris of his own monotony.

A balding gentleman and his wife join.
And the loner activates himself, once again,

"Who is this gentleman?
Is he a creature haunted by his
wornness?
Or daunted by the sheepish
manaueability of the buxum lady

whose beauty he wedded a week back?
Beauty stimulates.
She, a driving force."

The theme thaws.
Who would delve into their hegemonies,
undaunted wisdom,
obtruding wilderness,
wanton indulgences?
Uncompromising heterogeneities reach a
point of comatous homogeneities
and in a posture of kneeling,
erupt, repeatedly,
vigorously eluding
intolerant tolerances.
Asymmetrically.
Uniquely guarded secrets,
amid vulnerable talks of women.
There are pedagogues and
there are intellectuals,
and the sycophants,
with their scummy brains.

Their outpourings hang on the mirage
of their blindness,
on the gad,
with their
muddy movements.

That buxom woman,
her architectural contours,
lips, oversized, enveloping,
eyes, devilishly inviting,
a treat for connoisseurs, then,
a boring spinster, now,
wriggling her huge hips,

giggles,
with an air of abstraction.

Mr. S yells,
"Wives have most ugly perception of
most beautiful things."
Ms S dancing with a young, uncouth chap.

Sublime beauties adventuring into arenas
hitherto unknown to them,
bringing one set of thoughts to the front,
winnowing the other
that they sumptuously laid to rest,
while uniquely matching their sublimity.
Gracious movements divulged intellective
abstractions,
facts too hard to come to sudden halt,
speculations too soft to be mopped up,
shimmering thoughts too canny to be opaque.
Those yearning associations confirming
modalities of unrevealed intents,
unruly confusions,
untruly made confessions
bid an adieu to me.

The casks stones live in
are valued casks.
They are psyched out of
the casks they live in.
Stillness of darkness taxies in.

Mr Narcissus enters.
What a grand entry, our very own, most revered,
brainy Mr Narcissus, a man of great intellect, and intuition,
(at least he firmly believes in it)
makes his noble appearance, accompanied by
huge, moving baskets of flesh and bones.

Two very hefty women, I mean, relatively young,
Mr Narcissus so fond of.
"Whan...t? ...Oh my Gosh... Whan...t"
That old spinster caught unawares, the same nasal voice.

Chorus,

"Women talk of men who matter,
men talk of women who matter,
they grope together, in tandem,
as if the face of reason is tattered.
Unrolling their designs
the dreamers whisper along,
for one dream would crush
so many others, of others."

"An old wine in new bottle."
Mr Narcissus tells the two fat ladies.

What moves there? I mean in that group.
Mad rush.
Or
Madness running amuck.
Muse and its resonance,
silently viewing their death.
Ruse overwhelms muse.
The rescuer, crowded in the
confusion of his own,
breathes heavily, uttering nonchalantly,
"So what."

Fossilized arguments flow like
reckless cards crumble down.
Perforated faces get more perforated
as arguments begin seeking fullness.

That loner emerges again from hidden corners,

"Mr W.B. Yeats,
your times, your poetic stars.
Beautiful times, beautiful stars.
Superfluous people, then,
"All shuffle there; all cough in ink", only.[4]
Different are our times, our stars,
Superfluous people, now, cough in routed weariness.
Our superfluous people relish the creeping
decrepitude,
everyone differs from the rest,
everyone holds his own,
as is superfluous people' wont.
Superfluous people dream the dreams
not only of their but of
others too.
Rare indeed.
Everybody helps everybody
else realizing his or her
dreams, the dreams that hang fire
since time immemorial.
Hard facts come staring at their face,
and their collective dreams usher into
sudden grief.
Real indeed."

Superfluous people, nearby, hear the loner,
and suddenly they cry,
in complete unison,

"Scholars have ceased to dream
now, for only cretins can
dream now."
How chaotically true, indeed?

Superfluous people differ, yet they agree,
they agree, yet they differ.

---

[4] W.B. Yeats in *The Scholars*.

Superfluous people determining
the fate of everything while
knowing nothing.

And thereby let their complete vision
mess up with all pervading confusions.
And again they talk of their own mission
duly incorporating their lavish ambitions.

The corridors are never emptied,
the stony walls stay heartless
as these are known to be,
the faces are split
like spilt-milk.

Superfluous people.
Magnificently activated, activities
bore complete meaninglessness
as if,
barren darkness slithers
as their barren intelligence convulses
on their blankness.

That loner, sorry, a long victim of this ongoing onslaught
on sensitivities and sensibilities,
again butts in,

"My dear, aloofness is no excuse.
Aloofness prolongs wait....
Insensitivity is no insensibility
nor insensibility is insensitivity.
I know chaps.
Still I would be a silent man
for, I believe in firmness of sound of
silence, a sound that kills the might of
thousands of senseless voices, heard daily,
everywhere....

Is deception the end of arrogance?
Or is it the beginning of ignorance?
Make out please, for yourself.
You, an element of the crowd.
crowd, subordinated crowd,
lost in scrambled image of
superfluous people."

A gnawing omnipotence, a bigger answer,
the biggest question,
a lewd joke, an unbelievable hubbub,
a disquieting shyness,
all roam around the
ignorance of the hollow expressions.

For fairly long time we are waiting
for things to happen here,
in this big hall,
long time you measure as years, as decades,
as centuries.
We rest our hopes on ourselves,
for we have taught ourselves to wait
and wait till eternities expire.

The soliloquist's time has come;
he leaves that big hall, in great hurry,
amid these lines—
"You are nothing but a set
Of obsolete responses. The one thing to do
Is to do nothing. Wait."[5]

We know where our wait would lead
us to,
perhaps to that land of desolation,
where the knot of torpidity would

---

[5] T.S. Eliot in *The Cocktail Party.*

absorb us slowly.
Yes we wait. All of us wait
to get the judgment
from an unexpected quarter.

Feelings

Feelings crowded in,
splintering of the feelings,
preciseness redefined.

Passiveness of feelings,
abject wilderness,
earnestness, veil with glosses.

Unfelt avalanche of dead feelings,
an escape into rawness,
dishevelment revisited.

Feelings, whispers of decay,
fierceness stirring,
spontaneity dissolves.

Feelings, traceless gems,
silence in salvation,
shuffled life, no grudge.

Shattered feelings unresolved,
best is worst, worst is best,
places altered, dignified.

Feelings beyond fopperies,
Resemblances, haphazard
elusive, elusive, elusive.

Escapist

Don't try to pack all things within your tiny
inaccessibility,
go beyond your fears,
and bring ease to your distresses.
This is what I think of you, my dear escapist,
the world is not so unkind, not so gloomy.
Much have you traveled in the realms of
unease and disquietude,
but have you ever seen the tranquility of morning,
the pleasures of evening,
the ascending credence of night.
The heart that once fainted and
the face that once grieved
are the heart and the face that
mutter to each other, now,
about your inescapability.
Their hopes.
What would happen to their hopes?
You have bowed before marshy
struggle within,
degenerating into ascending
unhappiness.
Come on, dear,
not totally impaired.
our moral frame still
breathes morally.

Phenomena

Part I

Phenomena don't explain relations;
you move within unresting cycle of
phenomena, riddled with nascent experiences.
Two ideas induce the third one;
irrespective of intellect and knowledge,
the third one representing neither loss
nor reconstruction.
Reason flows not from what we know,
cognitive process,
recurrence is no change,
our recurrences do imply neither
purity of wholeness
nor impurity of parts,
neither perceptual truths
nor perceptual falsity.
You exist at one moment
and cease the next,
recoiling from moments and moments,
reconciliation gets uprooted.
What seems to be shifting
is nothing but a phenomenon
within a phenomenon,
like belongings belonging to
what has entered into the realm of
becoming
or unbecoming.
You are, needlessly, afraid of
immobility of resting phenomena,
a collection of restless phenomena.
The otherness of the former,

a generalized extraction,
of the latter, a generalized deduction.
In memory and in imagination,
they come and they go,
with their usual disjointedness
and with their flat and heavy judgments,
confirming their self-existence.
Your concepts as your percepts,
behaving like immediateness of innerness,
signify unity of their imaginative certitudes,
sensibilities sit on awkward premises.

Squalid inananess
galloping inside
the inner terrain,
fused with inexplicable
sensations.
Allusions run amuck.
Portents of phenomena
transcended
in portents of
no phenomena.

Part II

Nothing searches creation
more harmoniously than the
questions seeking answers
in unruly eternity.
Nothing explains creation
more disharmoniously than
the answers that lie deep buried,
beneath sequestered veil of
the questions.
What begins and where,
none knows.
Who begins and how,

none knows.
How long does it take?
How far will it go?
Where will it end?
Will it?
Or
Will it not?
What goes inside?
What comes outside?
Where do they meet?
Who meets first?
Do they meet at all?
Do they tread alone?
Or
Do they not?
What stretches flat there,
smoothed-out?
Nothing.
Or perhaps something that
hallucinates both the beginning
and the end.
Who warms whose decadence?
Inspired by heavenly joy?
Inspired by hellish despair?
Does it reach the ethereal extremities?
Where does the flow halt?
And where does it freeze?
Where does it melt?
Elements of evocation waver.
Time is fragmenting.
And who embraces whose discontinuities?
Unknowable floats on knowable,
knowable on unknowable.
Intimacy.
Apartness.
What keeps shifting between the two?

Don't we glimpse through the
penumbra of creations nauseating
in our fascinating self-descriptions?
Do the above ecstatic uncertainties, timeless
uncertainties vie with each other
driving us to the unchartered land of
somnambulists, arguably busy in
thinking what creation is all about?

Part III

Matterless thoughts, full of forms,
knowledge without wisdom,
wisdom without knowledge,
moving themselves in an equal
measure.
What you call void and what you call
full happen to be full and happen to
be void;
phenomena, creation all happening
and unhappening all the time.

Phenomena have just begun.
End has just ended.
Beginning ends before end begins.
End elopes with beginning.

Connectivity

Life,
a broken affair,
death
a complete affair.
One
loyal,
the other
royal.
Life,
a fumbling journey,
death,
a culmination of flame.
One
a squeamish story,
the other
a listener in harmony.
Unshaped life
meets its
counterpart
in
shaped death.
We are ahead
of the game,
life plays with death,
everything else meaningless.
Ponderous portions
of life
lumber, searching
compactness of death,
everything else reawakened.
Life,

an unsanctified surface,
death,
oblivious of sleepless tranquility.
One
a mighty master once,
the other
the mightiest servant,
forever.

It

I look at things around me;
and failing to find it,
look inside things;
again failing to find it,
look into the portrait on the wall
and find it there, inside the glass,
smiling at the imperceptibility
of its faith.

I look at zenith and I look at nadir;
I look there and I look here,
failing to find it anywhere
I look at somewhere deep
inside, neither here nor there,
and that luminous messenger
stands there, lost in his profane love
for himself.

When hundred tales are told;
it spins off,
when no tales are heard,
it pulls itself out of hundred labyrinths
tales refuse to put forth.
I console myself.
Tales or no tales,
I wouldn't enter labyrinths,
for I would meet it, there.

It has a mystique around it,
it knocks
when none hears
and none responds;
it departs

when all hear
and all respond.

It remains unsaid,
defying that old, irrelevant
logic;
what is unsaid can never be
braided into a poem.

I would now move ahead,
despite you,
against my will,
to meet those image lines
you have harboured for me.

When a very little remains of you
I will come back to you
to walk over your nude smoothness,
to fill spaces.
I wouldn't trespass your realms.
I know your sense of imminence.
And you mine.

When it opens up
its unsteady weight becomes
an excessive burden on itself.
Inexorable anguish I see on your
face,
growing bigger and bigger,
pitilessly pathetic.

It now enters a relationship,
between
what was once terrible
and
what is now fascinating;
I resist that relationship.
Of no avail.

That relationship
with it
returns back to me
like uprooted silence
striking me dead.

Unremembered People

Those, we don't cherish to remember,
come to us in our dreams;
midnight dreams,
knocking aloud,
these wanted/unwanted,
desired/undesired guests,
deadly intruders, sitting on fuzzy edges,
talk to us, laugh, eat with us,
play, oftentimes weep,
writhe in pains, quarrel with us,
and make our intense memory
ebb in our dreams.

They leave us,
amid the magnified meaning of life.
And in the magnified meaning of life
we are at cross-purposes with our negatives
unable to live with them,
or without them,
as if we have lived totally
meaningless life like water
that has never warbled.

Temple And Tavern

We have not heard for very long
those beautiful songs
that once enlightened us.
Not because the temples are not there,
temples have become breathless,
we are solaced more in taverns than
in temples.
In the latter, we see gods in varying forms
seeking themselves variously
toying with an undisguised soul,
in the former, we seek others in one form
knowing not what we seek about.
In temple a beginning stays a beginning,
in tavern everything begins and
nothing ends.
The endless bliss.

Shadows And Lost Relations

I

My euphoria stays, undiminished;
within my loneliness,
dreaded as well as desired,
as she came when I needed her:
And you uplifted my sagging spirits;
my morale being at such a low ebb.

II

From the very beginning,
a thought tortures me, pains me,
my fear of losing the relations I cherish to evolve.
I fear, one day, on that path, not visible now, but I see it,
clearly, very clearly,
as I bulldoze my way through this visibility
I will be walking through an array of
shadows that once illumined
my thought processes, that once transhumanized me, that
once cleared my conscience;
but now itself these shadows ask me the questions for which
I have responses but very obsolete ones only.
You speak about loneliness.
For thousand and thousand
of years,
I am alive in this jungle of
loneliness.
The jungle, enmeshed in me.
This loneliness is dear to me as
amid this loneliness
I meet a few who add pain to my
loneliness and leave;

a pain that I will pour unto myself
when you emerge as a verity in my
mind/imagination.

III

I feel the fluidness of these shadows,
I also feel that the waves of these shadows will break
into unpredictable cycles
and these unpredictable cycles will further fragment into
questions.
What will I really do, then?
Realization has its own cost.
Perhaps I never realize it,
I never conceptualize it, never
anticipate it, never idealize it.
I fear those who leave me,
for good.
Then I don't feel pain.
If loneliness does not have pain
embedded into it,
then there will be no loneliness,
no pain.

IV

Flatness of shadows is what I am irked at,
these flat shadows really mean a lot to me,
these reflect my relations in a mirror
when darkness is complete and
"Both of lost happiness and lasting pain
Torments *me*; ...
....
The dismal situation waste and wild;"[1]
and that mirror sleeps, an extraordinary sleep,
an irresponsible sleep, an incontrovertible sleep.

---

[1] Milton in *Paradise Lost*—1–55 to 60. (italics mine)

So my relations have no full reflection for me.
Time's greatest strength, I mean,
forgetfulness does not pity me,
so unfortunate it has been to me so far.
My coldness judges me and my relations from unrecognized
angles, I will not be able to explain these now
but I have no explanations, now, nor will I ever have.
I am a shock-less creature,
shocks have become incapacitated,
I will never recite those poems that keep the keys of
my lost relations to themselves.
How can I?
I have no keys.
You went away with my keys.

V

I grope inside inward sphere.
and observe.
And if what I observe does not happen,
my loneliness will desert me;
jungle will be abolished,
abolished will be I.
For thousand and thousand of years
you would keep coming to me.
Perhaps this trust of mine enlivens
my this very moment.
There, very far off, stands my destination
like an undulating star,
where one day I will stand, as usual,
alone with a wait...wait and...wait.
Sooner or later,
I will be in a strange whirlpool,
a whirlpool that neither
will let me in or out,
for at the door, ajar,
will sit my feelings;

my emotions,
alive and fresh,
dried and dead.
That is the pain of loneliness,
that is the pain of a memory
that refuses to part with,
leaving a zigzag of "moral sense",
"passions", "affections"
"self-love", "self-interest",
"natural affections","un-natural"
emotions/feelings behind.[2]
Someday, unknown, unseen
unheard, unfelt,
these feelings will tell me the themes
that I will play with,
as I always do,
when my loneliness unwraps me.
And at this unearthly hour of
this dark, halting night
I visualize that someday
when what I play with will give me
an intellectually autonomous milieu
where only both of us will rejoice
the idea of separation,
as if we were never separated out, ever.

VI

I hope someday these poems will realize my sorrow,
the sadness

[2] The ideas developed by Lord Shaftesbury in his essay, Men, Manners, Opinions and Times concentrate on three kinds of human emotions/feelings: self-love and self-interest which he calls ethically neutral, first kind; unselfish, altruistic and benevolent feelings called natural affections, the second kind and emotions—vicious and malevolent which he calls, un-natural, the third kind. A poet has to carry, painfully, all these with him while retrieving emotions/feelings from memory when he writes.

of relations that are lost, midway,
never, perhaps, to be retrieved again,
and hand over the keys, at least once,
to enable me judge the depth of the cauldron of lost relations.
Now I am very tired, dead-tired.
I feel this.
I co-exist with lost relations, shadows, questions, a fate
I fall back, again and again,
in search of the shadows whose questions
I will be called upon to
honour in my dying hours of life
when a new life will be awaiting me
with another set of shadows,
another set of relations, another set
of questions and possibly
a fresh set of answers.
But, nay, nay,
I am not stupid.
I know the depths I have; the intensities
I have; these would take me to
yet another cycle of my life.

Iniquitous Survival

Unequalled
inequities,
stretching,
derision
and
glory;
making
excellent
bed
fellows.

No
shape,
no
significance,
no
flux,
no
impulses,
perpetual
war
continues.

Unsecured
persona
evolving
aimlessly.
Woes
of
time
conflict.

Guilt
mocking,
void,
entering
primitive
impulses.
Errorless
follies
smile,
jejunely.

Strangers
come,
stay,
depart,
leaving
unreal
ignorance
of
real
fears.

Troubled
by
guilt,
glittering
conscience
leaves
nothing
to
us.

Strains,
voyage
to
inferno,
parts
strung-out.

Made
less
forlorn,
our
glimpses
marveled
at.

You
survive,
I
survive,
we,
iniquitous
partners,
standing
with
our passed days.

An Evening In That Tavern (1980)

6 P.M.
I have reached, once again,
through my memory
that has coaxed me, as is its wont,
to go to that place, that time
the tavern,
I thought, then, miracles were not perfected
in such places, in such times;
such being the pain to be in two exclusions,
faith and truth hugging each other
like two boozers measuring each other's
nocturnal brightness.
Who wins and who loses?

Our arguments go after themselves,
slowly and steadily,
reasons meet their own end here;
illogic broods sagaciously
over the drowsing words of loathsome
inhumanity.

Now, faraway from you, in this strange world,
ruled by silent unease,
I draw a line and sit on it for hours, long hours
(6 P.M.—11 P.M.)
buttonholing what I lost when I left you amid
your cold, lemony sighs of despondence.
Pondering over incongruity of my thoughts,
I visit
the street, narrow, harrowing,
the tavern, absorbing, drowsing,

thirsty lips/thirstier evenings,
the large, dark eyes,
their talks, loud and lewd,
telling me
about the annoyed joys of life,
an unfaithful friend, abandoned love, lost honour
fragmented beauty and lusty dreams.

Here, I learn
liberated souls look at the daybreak and gossip
about clustering dawn.
liberated souls look at the daybreak and rejoice
staleness of the ensuing dusk.

The lanterns relishing their extinguished, almost
extinguished images,
having been lit in their own chillness,
the urchins howling about the hunger,
their only inheritance.
When the moon was dark, stars irreversible,
when the sun was bleak, earth reversible,
I slept in your lap upset by my own trepidation,
and waiting for yours.
Shy evasive birds sang throughout and
the crows and the dogs made noise as usual,
the hooting owls ruled the roost as usual,
but did you ever tell me to succumb.
Never.
With you and you alone,
I saw an indecent burial of the corpse,
I saw an indecent meal being served,
I saw worn out clothes sobering us,
I saw her dying coolly, patiently and happily,
I saw the lepers playing with the stray dogs,
loving them, cajoling them,
I saw my parents lost somewhere,
I saw my teachers quarrelling with their poverty,

I saw my beloved retreating far-off,
enchanting me with what she never promised me.
I penned my name and then hers
side by side
on that old banyan tree,
that I expected would live for yet another
1000 years.

I wish I could have seen an unheard sigh.
I wish I could have heard an unseen music.
I wish I could have felt an unfelt warmth.
I wish I could have unfelt a felt darkness.

Still you were so good, for
I saw decent, honest, elderly tears
rolling down your cheeks,
I saw dead images,
upraised in terrestrial darkness,
moaning mercilessly in empty places.
And in your withdrawn enigma,
we, drunkards, dribbled towards each other,
augmenting our self-respect
and killing our illusions.
We searched our own language
unfurled our invisibilities,
unearthed limitless absence of faith
in the vapid idols emerging from
obdurate depths of yours.

Now, here, the ruling ghosts make me
stronger and stronger
telling me mildly but firmly
of nuances of
stories, inimical,
you solemnly forgot to tell on my
leaving you.
Scintillating memories draw a parallel between

what have faded completely
and what are on the
verge, but I kept sitting on the line,
in this wild stony place,
searching for impatient,
dispersing hailstone of whitened joys,
yet to come.

The fabricating rays of light
indignantly infuse
fallibility into infallibility,
unmindful of bruises.

And lo and behold!
There, these come,
symmetrically, some times,
asymmetrically, some times,
darkening stars walking on,
dancing, leaping, galloping,
bringing with them perturbing
brightness,
jubilantly.

Who wins and who loses?
We don't know.
Then let our past answer this.
That very past hanging over our shoulders in a timeless,
motionless
hiatus of unfilled flaws.

And a new dawn and a new dusk
await on the horizon
that rests on gliding hopelessness.
6 A.M.

And The Budding Poetess Averred, "Word is memory; memory word"

Fragrance of words enlivens
the dead fragrance of feelings.
Fragrance of words enlivens
the dead fragrance of reasons.
Inside their seclusion, the words
seize neither the beginning of the end
nor the end of what never
begins.
And words change; their meanings change,
the emotions change; the sentiments change,
as changes time and as changes memory.
Words are day and words are night,
words are dark and words are light.
But, you ought not forget this;
"The change of the word does not
alter the matter."[1]
Really.
Inside the fortress of shattered
frustrations, the words seize
themselves, stubbornly, in order
to search intensity of meanings
into what they are not.
Fragrance of traceless words
now rejoices at its own victory,
for the feelings and the reasons
have successfully slaved both
the wakefulness and the dream.

---

[1] From Sir Thomas More's *Utopia*. Conversation between Raphael and Peter on Peter's advice to Raphael to join any King's service.

That is memory.
Sliced words queer the kindred
craving for the dead expectations,
hoping that the hatred for silent
sympathy halts for a while.
Immemorially outrageous words
fog the paling away of their
meanings that lay buried deep
down remorseful years.
Words never determine what is simple,
what complex, as
"there are no tricks in plain and simple faith."[2]
The artists who once created the
boundaries of varied words now
see the glory of their art perishing
melancholily.
The hues, humid and roseate,
the grace, fulfilling and tuneful,
the grandeur, sublime and ethereal,
the clues, blossoming and eddying,
desert the words in the whirlwind
of their melodious plight.
Words have their own pangs.
The redeemer chooses to enliven
the memories that are drowsing,
unable to retrieve the wraths of memory.
The redeemer chooses to survey
the delusions, bordering with
absolute senility.
The redeemer chooses to erase
the betrayals, sane people, their words
give to memories.
Rehashed hypocrisies forbid the
recurrence of logical cogitations that

---

[2] Brutus in *Julius Caesar* (Act 4-scene II).

have jangled, wearing hamous
scars but have continued treading
the path of illogical ruminations.
Languid future broods stubbornly
as melancholies vie with each other
in order to prove their proven
superiorities.
Mad responses are bewildering.
Pimpled reactions are bewitching.
Rootless sagas are slow.
Stratified emotions are screaming.
There is neither word
nor memory.
Words are dark and words are light;
You tell me: not all things need be said.
Of what use silence is if it has no words.
I am no Orphic saint[3]; words are, would
always be.
Hence, your silence I wouldn't interpret;
I am indifferent; words are not; words
are memory; memory is not.
Dark trembles light.
Light trembles itself.
Words tremble everything
and is there anything trembling
words?
The two extremes really don't matter
now, for the centre of that invisible, unknown
territory deceitfully has created so many
centers/sub-centers where words enjoy the pain
of their fringes
and I want to be left all alone, perhaps with,

---

3 Orphism, the very early system of Greek Philosophy believed that there were Orphic saints who had pre-existed their birth and would exist after their death, and hance are immortals.

"a fear of vacuum, and no desire to fill it."[4]
I feel, this fear of mine would soon fill
the vacuum with words, self-explanatory words
but not confusing words; words that confuse make
bad memories or no memories;
and bad memories or no memories leave a sad
history behind, none will be proud of.
But I, as always, trust your words;
"Even now, I am proud of our relations."
Those, proud of relations,
don't experiment with these;
they trust and render a happiness;
a unique happiness to both
word and memory
that combine to make relations.

---

[4] T.S. Eliot in *The Elder Statesman.*

What some of the Poets/International Review Writers say of Srivastava's First book *Ineluctable Stillness*

"In this collection, Srivastava insists on the unstated, the implicit and the fragmentary.... One of the most striking aspects of the poems is Srivastava's delight in the musical dimension of poetry. He uses poetry to create a free self-positive, humane, fully exposed to life. He has made some of life's most important and most challenging topics accessible even to those readers without a strong background in philosophy or moral dilemmas."

Patricia Prime,
New Zealand

"This is poetry drawing us to a new look at new forms which attract us to read, continue reading until devoured. The depths of his work enlighten us, draw us to want to read his future endeavors with pleasure."

Rosemary C. Wilkinson
President Emeritus World Congress of Poets,
U.S.A.

"The beauty of the poetry of Mr K.K. Srivastava's is not a familiar sight. It produces the feelings that one gets after visiting unfamiliar sights.... He writes poetry that is individual in it's subject and individual in it's style. It appears that basically Srivastava is a thinker and this aspect comes out clearly in his poetry."

Dr Stephen Gill
Ansted Poet Laureate and
Noble Prize Nominee for Literature,
Canada

Srivastava's book is "intellectually challenging"..."well-ordered, free verse poetry, unique in style, rhythmical in cadence and so delightfully alliterative in word-play." Some of his "longer poems have distinct echoes of T.S. Eliot's *The Waste Land*, with perhaps an added flavouring of the playwright Samuel Beckett...."

Bernard M. Jackson,
U.K

"Srivastava's poems are not only beautiful, they are really strong with a great clarity of thought."

Prof. Kurt F. Svatek,
Austria

"He is not a genteel poet, he is a disturbing poet, intent on unraveling the human mind of its false preconceptions, of it's delusive hypocrisy masked as genuine emotions."

Hindustan Times

"Srivastava's rare qualities as a writer come to the fore in the poems which are mature expressions of both in form and style. He has proved his hands in toeing the traditional meters. His choice of diction is very nice. The symbols and images he evokes to give vent to his emotions are beautiful. He exhibits the traits of Shiv K. Kumar in his verses."

Poetcrit

"Srivastava is at his best in his longer poems which notwithstanding their droning prolixity possess a striking sweep of force and poetic fire...bringing his talent bear upon his lines skillfully just as ingeniously he develops his theme."

Sahitya Akademi's
Indian Literature

"Human emotions with their varied outbursts, of course intellectually and poetically conceived by the poet are to be understood in serene atmosphere with patience. The deep sense of humanity at higher level of cosmopolitan conscience is wedded in the lines of the verses."

Contemporary Vibes

"Very splendid, very thoughtful book.... I have the first impression that Srivastava is a very philosophical personality thinking of his own life and that of others in a very accurate and careful way...poems are not very easy to understand by broad public."

Dr Carla Kraus,
Vienna

"His poetry sounds differently and eccentric. He has many identity reflections...a social commentator and a psychologist of words."

Mbizo Chirasha,
Zimbabwe